Writing a BOOK *God's Way in* 100 DAYS

Writing a BOOK *God's Way in* 100 DAYS

Earma Brown
Inner Court Publishing

Writing a BOOK *God's Way* *in* 100 DAYS

Published by Inner Court Publishing
An imprint of Butterfly Press

ISBN 978-0-9797701-7-3
Published in the United States of America

Cover Design: ScribereCreative.com

EPIGRAPH

One generation will commend your works to another;
they will tell of your mighty acts. —Psalm 145:4

DEDICATION

This book is dedicated to the Broadway Family:

Oneadia Kates, Marie Toms, Cecelia Tasby,
Marilyn Worsham, Lenner Broadway, Jr., Linda Howard,
Minnie Broadway and Bernard Broadway.

Thank you for believing in me.

TABLE OF CONTENTS

How to Use This Book xi

Chapters

1. How to Write a Book God's Way In 100 Days 15

2. Selecting a Topic That Sells 29

3. Mapping Your Book Journey With a Plan 41

4. Designing Passion Points to Sell Way More 57

5. Developing a Promotion Plan Before Chapter 1 69

6. Giving Your Book the Test of Significance 83

7. Sizzling Titles Sell Way More Than Dud Titles 99

8. Mining the Gold Called Your Knowledge 113

9. How to Build a Saleable Book 125

10. Finishing Your Book Faster and Selling Sooner 137

11. How to Write Compelling C.H.A.P.T.E.R.S. 155

12. How to Create Multiple Income Streams 169

Report 1. How to Turn Your Book Into An Ebook 181

Report 2. Self Publishing 101 189

Appendix I: WABGW Writing Commitment Form 199

Appendix II: 25 Book Writing Strategies 201

Appendix III: 100 Day Book Writing Timeline 203

About the Author 205

Other Resources 207

HOW TO USE THIS BOOK

Dear Aspiring Author:

Welcome to the *Writing a Book God's Way In 100 Days* 12 week training! I'm excited to have you as a valued member of our *Book Writing Course* training program; I am looking forward to seeing your "book" come to life over the next few days and weeks.

This book was created as a companion course book for the *BookWritingCourse.com* membership site but it can be used as a stand alone study guide with practical exercises to write your book manuscript to completion.

Before we begin with the inaugural lesson, there are some important things that I need to mention to you...This book was specifically designed for aspiring Christian authors. You have a special place in my heart.

I seek to inspire and encourage you as a believer to write for His glory. By receiving this book you have gained a friend and a coach in your corner. I've taken what I usually pour into one-on-one book coaching and distilled it into this book.

As a friend I will encourage you and offer valuable tips on how to get your book completed faster but in excellence. As a coach in your corner, you can expect me to push you to the discipline needed to complete your book.

It has taken me many years to learn the core writing principles. Years ago, our Father God comissioned me as His writer. Under His direction and guidance I've written over 10 books, scores of ebooks and a host of articles through the years.

Now I get the privilege of sharing some of those lessons with you in a course format. I'm a teacher at heart; I hope you have as much fun as I did in putting this book together for you. One more thing, if you already have a copy of the *Write Your Best Book Now: How to Write a Book In 100 Days or Less* course book or taken the online course then you have the core principles.

Special Invitation:

1) You are invited to enroll in the *BookWritingCourse.com* membership website. Sign-up now at, http://www.bookwritingcourse.com/specialoffer.htm and you will receive a special discount and time released bonus reports designed for the *Writing A Book God's Way In 100 Days* book owners only.

As a member of this course site, you will receive 1 lesson per week via email and at least once per month, you'll automatically receive a FREE bonus as an active Book Writing Course™ subscriber. These bonuses will appear in your inbox approximately every 30 days and will include accessories and training materials to further focus your book writing and even create extra profit streams for you.

2) Additionally, as a subscriber you will receive some built-in surprises (templates, tools, coaching, etc.) along the way at unspecified intervals. And, finally, there is a SUPER "graduation" bonus at the completion of your 3-month training that is literally worth more than the quarter's subscription dues ... so look for that on graduation day.

3) What's inside this book? So glad you wanted to know! Here's a quick look at what we'll cover during the 12 lessons in your training and the bonus reports you have received already just by getting a copy of this book…

- Lesson #01: Jumpstart - How to Write a Book God's Way In 100 Days
- Lesson #02: Pillar 1 - Preparation: Selecting a Book Topic That Sells

- Lesson #03: Pillar 2 - Planning: Mapping Your Book Journey with a Plan
- Lesson #04: Pillar 3 - Passion Points: Designing Passion Points to Sell Way More Books
- Lesson #05: Pillar 4 - Promotion: Developing a Promotion Plan before Chapter 1
- Lesson #06: Giving Your Book the Test of Significance
- Lesson #07: Sizzling Book Titles Sell More Books
- Lesson #08: Mine the Gold Called Your Knowledge
- Lesson #09: How to Build a Saleable Book
- Lesson #10: Finishing Your Book Faster and Selling Sooner
- Lesson #11: How to Write Compelling C.H.A.P.T.E.R.S.
- Lesson #12: How to Build Multiple Streams of Income
- Bonus Lesson 1 How to Turn Your Book Into an Ebook!
- Bonus Lesson 2 Self Publishing 101

You may have noticed; the first month will be the basic steps involved in getting your book writing off to a good but quick start and the next month will be all about structuring and writing an easy-to-read book for your potential readers.

Don't worry those that already have the basics covered; I've got some "golden nuggets" in these preliminary lessons for you as well! So don't tune out; you'll miss some important ideas. Finally, the last few lessons and the bonus lessons are about preparing your manuscript to publish and produce more than one income stream.

4) Why You Should Not Stop Before You Finish. There are many reasons why you should stick with your course (It's great training; if you keep quitting one thing and going to another you'll never get your book done, even if you don't use it all now you can archive it to use later, etc.)

CHAPTER 1

How To Write A Book God's Way In 100 Days

Teach us to number each of our days so that we may grow in wisdom.
—Psalm 90:12

In the first lesson, I give you some powerful points that will help you get your book started and completed. Implement these tips in your plan early and in 100 days or less you could have your manuscript written.

What if you discovered there was one little word that stood between your book dream being realized in the next 100 days or not? Would you want to know that one word? Yes, great! Before I tell you, think about this.

There are thousands of people that die each year with their book dream never realized. You may wonder, what's the difference between the ones that die with a book inside them and the ones that put pen to paper to write a book?

Some say book authors have more smarts and more time. Perhaps they have a bigger brain or were born with a silver spoon in their mouth. None of the above is true. In fact, there's very little difference between the two groups. That little difference can be boiled down to one word, ACTION.

Both groups of authors receive great ideas and inspired

messages. One group receives the idea but never ACTS on it. They never develop it and it eventually fades away. The group that fulfils their dream of becoming an author receives the idea, ACTS on it, develops it and completes it. Won't you join the group that acts on their ideas? Here are 7 tips that will help you write a book in the next 100 days or less:

1. **Move your book dream up to the top 3 priorities.** No, you don't have to sell your soul anymore to write a saleable book. Instead, use the cumulative effect of doing a little bit at a time. Even so, unless you want it to take years to write, you must schedule writing time each week. For example, you could write 2 pages a day and have a short book in weeks.

   Develop a regular writing schedule. Think about your priorities right now. Can you fit 15-20 hours a week in? If you have to let something go that is not high on your priority list, do it. Now is your time. Next year is not better. Set yourself up for a successfully written book in the next 100 days by making your book goal a top priority.

2. **Stamp out the fear of failure.** Many writers tremble in their tracks with fear that their book won't sell. Don't be afraid. Your book will sell if its presents useful information, answers important readers questions, and impacts people for the good. If it presents entertaining or humorous information it could go farther than you imagined.

   If it creates a deeper understanding of humanity, animals of this world its worth reading. With one to three of these elements your book is worth writing. More than three, it has potential of making great sales –even to best seller status. Go ahead, write your book and make the world a better place. (Test your book in chapter 6.)

3. **Know who will buy your book.** In other words, choose your target audience. Then write your book for them. When you give your book a target, it will resonate with your audience. To be honest, your book will not interest everyone. When you target one audience at a time, each tip, each story or how-to will be more effective. Aim your message and you will have a competitive edge on most book writers.

   For many just shoot their message out into the dark and hope it connects with someone. When targeting your potential readers, create an audience profile. Are your potential readers male or female? How old are they? Are they interested in self-help, mystery, romance, how-to books? What problems do they face? Are they business people or professionals? Are they techies or non-techies? Are they willing to spend $15-30 on your book?

QTip: The core process located at the end of this chapter are organized in chronological order for your convenience.

<u>DECIDE upon a targeted market and topic.</u>

A "market" consists of a wide group of people with a specific related interest that you'd like to sell your book to. Examples include: business marketing, health and fitness, college, self help, relationships, parenting, etc. A "topic" would be a subject to which the market is passionate, concerned or attracted. Examples include: affiliate marketing, losing weight, managing time, keeping romance alive, getting a grant for college, raising godly children, etc.

4. **Write your book's thesis.** Did you cringe at the word thesis? For some, it brought back memories of English class and writing essays. No worries, a thesis simply

reflects the main central thought of the book. Make sure the main central thought includes the greatest benefit of your book and you're done.

In other words, it should answer your audiences' question, "How will this book help, encourage or solve my problem for me?" Writing the thesis before you write the book will keep you on the path of focused, powerful yet easy to read content.

All chapters support your book's main concept. For the book "Write Your Best Book Now" the thesis is "How to write, complete, and publish your best book fast." The best titles often include the thesis statement in some form.

5. **Create your book's working title.** In the literary world it's called a *working title* because everyone knows it could and probably will change. You may decide to change it or your publisher. Even so, working titles help direct and focus your writing.

   Some non-fiction writing does better with subtitles. If needed, it clarifies the title. Clever titles may sound cute but if confusing, they will miss the mark and sales.

   Which titles grab you and stir a desire to read what the author has to say: "Rich Dad, Poor Dad: What the Rich Teach Their Kids About Money - That the Poor and Middle Class Do Not!" or "How to Teach Others About Money." Another re-worked title is, "How to Win Friends and Influence People!" or "How to Make Friends."

6. **Make an inspiration cover early.** Keep it by your desk to inspire you. Book covers are the number one selling point of a book. Of course, in the beginning this is only a working cover. Nevertheless it will help crystallize your thoughts and propel you toward the fulfilment of

your dream. Remember, you have about 4-10 seconds to impress your audience to buy.

Browse the bookstores and the Internet to get a few ideas. Study the covers best suited for your audience. Choose colours that attract them. Consider blue and red for business books; aqua, yellow, and shades of red work for personal growth books. Avoid using too much red; it makes many feel suspicious.

7. **Write the back cover as sales message before you write your book.** This benefit driven outline helps give your book direction and helps you focus on what's really important to your readers. Most books will only allow for 50-75 words. That gives you about 8-20 seconds to impress your prospective buyer. Make this message passionate. Include only what sells: reader and famous testimonials, a benefit driven headline to hook the reader to open the book and read the table of contents, and bulleted benefits.

8. **Compose your book's 60 second "commercial" before you begin writing.** Have you heard a 60 second radio commercial recently? The information is distilled into sound bytes to be effective. Make your 2-3 sentence book blurbs into a sound byte. Like a radio commercial where you only have a few seconds to get your message across, condense your sound byte into a 60 second tell and sell.

   Use your mini commercial at networking meetings, in the elevator, in the grocery line, anywhere you only have a few seconds to tell about your book. Composing your short commercial should include your book title and 3 top benefits.

9. **Create and organize your book files.** Researchers say we waste over 150 hours a year looking for misplaced information. Create an organization method that fits you. For example, to save time and get organized you can create a master folder with your book's title. Inside, keep a separate file for each chapter. Assign each chapter a short title that will make sense later. If you don't have a title then assign names by topic.

   Put research notes or resources in each chapter named folder. Make a how-to folder as well, such as short-key notes, style or formatting notes. With this system you can manage multiple projects easily. Stop wasting time with disorganized, unfinished projects; get rid of methods that don't produce and help you get your message out in speed and excellence.

10. **Create your chapter's template or format**. Readers enjoy easy-to-read maps to guide them through your book. They love consistency. It is disconcerting and unprofessional if you change formats throughout the book. In non-fiction books, except chapter one, each chapter should be similar length and have same sections or categories. To make your chapters come alive, use engagement tools such as anecdotes, your case stories, sizzling headings, photos, maps, graphs, exercises, short tips. Readers enjoy easy-to-read side bars and pull quotes in boxes.

11. **Avoid re-inventing the wheel.** Use the information you already have. Your audience is looking for solutions to their problems. They are looking to you for encouragement to overcome their challenges. Mine your background, your files, and your speeches for the gold called <u>your knowledge and experiences</u>. Use speedy book writing techniques and

finish your book faster to sell sooner. Stay with what you know best, if possible.

You're the expert. To have the best chance to get your book done in the next 100 days, use what you have already written with small blocks of research, if needed. Use your speeches, your seminars, your notes and experiences. Fill your book with your stories, case studies and examples.

12. **Make an educated choice about your publishing options** before you write your book. Will you self-publish or shop for a traditional publisher? There are serious pros and cons for either method. Find out the differences so you can make an educated choice that suits you. If you are self-publishing, consider the POD technology for your book. There are lots of good choices that will publish your book for you at an affordable price.

    If you are opting for a traditional publisher, get an agent and a contract before writing the book. Then shop agents and publishers with 2-3 chapters and a knock-out book proposal. Invest in one of the current market guides and research the best fit for your work. It raises your chances considerably, if you know what kind of manuscripts a particular company is looking for.

Don't let one word keep you from realizing your book dream in less than 100 days. ACT now; you can do it. Remember to put your book writing in the top 3 priorities of your life, stump out fear of failure, know who will buy your book and write your book's thesis.

Then create your book's working title, develop an inspiration cover early, write in your passion points, organize your book files, create your chapter template, avoid re-inventing the wheel, and make an educated choice about your publishing options. Using the above simple tips you can easily write and complete your book in a 100 days or less. ACT now and use your ideas before they fade. Here's to your best success as Author!

4 PILLARS TO JUMPSTART WRITING YOUR BOOK

There are four "pillars" of writing a saleable book: *Preparation, Planning, Passion Points and Promotion.* Each of these is a necessary component in getting your book started the profitable way. If you were building a house they would, in essence, be your foundation.

1. *Preparation.* In the "preparation" stage you will make important decisions regarding your book: market selection, choosing a topic, getting to know your potential readers.
2. *Planning.* In the "planning" stage you will discover the difference between your marketing plan and your book proposal. You will in essence create a map for your book journey. Later in the course, I'll show you how to write a query letter and create a 1 page book proposal.
3. Passion Points. In the "passion point" stage you will discover how to make sure each selling point of your book is designed to sell. At each selling point your potential reader encounters, he or she is usually making a decision about your book whether it's to buy it or keep reading. You will discover how to compel them to buy or keep reading to the end.
4. *Promotion.* In the "promotion" stage you will plan how you are going to get the word out about your new book and attract your initial readers, as well as develop an ongoing marketing presence to continually funnel new sales and profits on your book journey.

We'll cover each of these in-depth over the next four lessons.

For now, let's identify the core process to complete successfully writing a saleable book (Visit the resource section at the back of this book or the http://bookwritingcourse.com website for printable strategies, lists and timelines.) You can use the 25 strategies and/or the 100 day timeline to jumpstart your book writing all the way to the finish line.

Whether you take the fast track or go step by step through the course lessons, can you grasp this? With the preparation and planning included you could literally be 100 days or less away from completing your book!

And, truthfully, it probably won't take that long for most people. After all, when you get your preparation and planning done it's only a matter of writing the information gleamed from your existing body of knowledge or research into the blank chapter templates you will create later!

So, let's go over the core process 1 quick time...

1. Use quick start techniques early

2. Select your book topic and get to know your potential reader.

3. Write a plan for what you want to do with your book.

4. Write your selling points before writing chapter 1.

5. Plan how you will promote your book before writing chap. 1.

6. Test your book's significance.

7. Develop title writing skills and create a sizzling title

8. Pull and organize info from your knowledge base, experience and/or research.

9. Create a table of contents & chapter template

10. Use speed techniques to finish faster and profit sooner.

11. Write compelling C.H.A.P.T.E.R.S. and/or rough draft manuscript.

12. Plan multiple streams of book income.

13. Create 1 Information Product from your book.

14. Consider self publishing basics.

That's all there is to it. And in terms of writing courses, it really doesn't get easier than this.

Now, before I mention this week's assignment, let me reiterate this one more time: This first lesson is an "overview" lesson. It is intentionally designed that way. It is purposeful. I've arranged it so experienced writers (or those that have already selected topics, etc.) can get started immediately and beginners can get a general idea of what we'll cover over the next 3 months.

In the next few lessons, I'll expound on a few things and give beginners baby-steps to complete each of the things we've talked about so far. Then, I'll also include some powerful insights for our advanced writers, especially in bonus lessons & lessons #6-10. Visit the back of the book in the resource section or the website http://bookwritingcourse.com for extra strategies and the *100 Day* timeline. Sign up for your free access to these printable resources and more.

Now, on to this week's assignment...

=======

WABGW
Book Writing Commitment

I [ ] prayerfully dedicate the next 100 days of my life to writing a book manuscript while using the resources I have to use (right now).

Print Name

Sign Name Date

Begin to act boldly. The moment one definitely commits oneself, heaven moves in his behalf. –Gerald R. Ford

THIS WEEK'S ASSIGNMENT

1) Copy the commitment statement; (located in resource section at end of book) fill it in and pin it up in your personal space. Make sure it's where you can see it daily or at least weekly. If you don't won't to rip page out of your book, sign-up at website www.bookwritingcourse.com to download free resources.

2) If you are an "experienced" student, *get started immediately writing your own book by following the 4 Pillar Quick Start Checklist, 25 Book Writing Strategies and/or Fast Track Module.* You should be well on your way in a couple of weeks or less. Obviously, in the course we'll tweak your plans to make sure your book is the most easy to read, saleable book during the coming weeks and months of our training.

3) If you are a "beginner" student, begin brainstorming ideas: possible topics for your book and possible markets. We've included a detailed module on choosing your topic in next week's lesson, but I'd like you to begin brainstorming some ideas for yourself at this point.

4) Develop and commit to a writing schedule. And get started this week. Wait you're not done, put it on a piece of nice paper and post it in your dressing or work area so you can see it every day:

Mon_____ Tue_____ Wed_____ Thu_____ Fri_____ Sat_____
Sun_____

WORDS WORTH REMEMBERING:

Commit your way to the LORD, trust also in Him,
and He shall bring it to pass. —Psalm 37: 5 (NKJV)

Coming Up Next ...

Chapter #2:

Pillar 1: Preparation – Selecting a Book Topic That Sells

In the next lesson we'll cover some key decisions in starting your book writing project such as targeted market selection and topic selection. If you already have your topic chosen, we'll discuss a unique angle for it so you can sell even more books.

CHAPTER 2

Selecting A Topic That Sells

The intelligent man is open to new ideas,
in fact he looks for them.
—Proverbs 18:15

In this chapter, I cover the first pillar Preparation of book writing. I offer you some pointers on selecting a book topic that makes your book stand out in the crowded marketplace and sell.

Did you know there are about 1.5 million books in print at any one time in the United States alone? Furthermore, there are over 195,000 new titles published each year in the United States.

Many aspiring authors feel their book would be lost in the sea of books already in print? May I be honest? That feeling is correct if you don't target your potential book readers well.

So, to choose your book topic and make it stand out in a crowd, you must write it for a targeted audience interested in your book's topic. Identifying a (niche) targeted audience is really hot in the marketing world right now and rightly so.

Simply put, to target a niche market or audience in your book's topic area: Identify a problem/solution and research your competition. Then develop a different approach. With all the books in the world on your topic, it's not enough to know the solution. You must present the solution in a different way than existing books do. Here are some of the things you can do first to select a book topic that stands out in the crowd and sells:

1. Allow your passion to guide you to a book topic. Choose a topic that will hold your interest for at least two years. Remember, your book is a part of you. Many authors call the book they wrote *their baby*. After all, if you're following this book writing program, your manuscript will be an accumulation of your speeches, your expertise and your research that you will birth. If you don't love your topic, you hinder your chances to be successful. No one will take an interest if you don't, so choose well.

2. Jot down 5 topics that ignite your passion. Ask your inner book writer which you should write first. If you're wondering how to do that, go sign-up for the *Book Writing Course* membership site for bonus reports including *Tap Into the Book Writer Inside* http://www.bookwritingcourse.com/specialoffer.htm

After choosing, organize your existing knowledge (everything you already know and want to know about that topic.) If you need more information on a topic, research it. Read related books in your field, interview existing experts in your field, review related web sites, and subscribe to newsletters. As you saturate yourself in this knowledge, you become the expert (if not already) as you write.

3. Create the magical pill. Write a book to fill the needs or desires of the people in your field. People look for solutions to their problems. In fact, most of us are looking for the *magic pill*. Make your book the *magic pill* by providing solutions to your reader's problems. The more intense the problem and the easier you can make your solution, the more readers will seek out your book.

Business books sell well. People are searching for help with specific skills such as writing, reading, speaking, computing, communication, math, sales, marketing and Internet. Non-fiction, self-help or how-to topics sell best. I encourage you to write a non-fiction book first. When you write a saleable non fiction title first, it can easily finance your other book projects.

4. Get to know your potential book readers. Research your selected market. You know, like who will buy your book? Solve a problem or offer insightful help and there will be many who will gladly pay the $14-$35 price of your book? An even better question is, "How does your book compare with your competition?"

What is your unique selling proposition? What personal benefits does your book offer its readers? The targeted market for the *Chicken Soup for the Teenage Soul* yielded three million more sales in one year than the original *Chicken Soup for the Soul* sold in three years. Select your targeted market well; it could be profitable!

5. Compare your book with other top selling books in your field. What way is your book like theirs? What makes your book different from others? How can you make your book better? Can you offer more detail. Can you make your more easy to read when others on the market are too complex. Is your book the only one of its kind? If it is, it could be more difficult to sell because mainstream buyers don't know about it.

To find out what category your book fits in, visit your local bookstore. Ask the bookseller to help you. Turn to the back covers and look at the upper left side to see the two or three categories usually listed there. Which ones does your book fit under? Let your book develop a new angle on the problem to be solved. A new weight loss book might sell way more copies when the author aims it at middle-aged women and calls it *Getting Fit at Fifty: Fabulous Ways to Become the New Forty*.

6. Survey your targeted market. Brainstorm with others. Ask for feedback from your writers group, your friends and colleagues. Connect with a book coach. Ask them to vote on the top ten titles, subtitles, chapter titles, and back cover information.

Your book title is the top 'Passion Point" designed to help sell your book after it's written. Any time spent on developing a sizzling title, you will not regret it. Your ideas multiply, exponentially, when you brainstorm with others. Additionally, don't become too attached to what you choose. Ideas from others always create a better book. We all have blind spots that will hinder us if we don't reach out.

7. Create a bigger dream for your book. In the new millennium, there's no excuse for your book to remain unpublished. If you're not famous already, tired of waiting for your big break or know someone at the top of the publishing industry, consider self publishing. Before you complete your book, specifically name the results you will experience (see, hear and feel.) Place these results (affirmations) along with the book title in color on a 3x5 card.

Position it near your workstation or on your bathroom mirror. Put it somewhere you will see it daily. Use the current date including the year: Now that my book (title and subtitle) is finished and is a huge seller. For example:

- *I see (smiling people at my speaking engagements buying it) or (hundreds of orders from my web site)*
- *I hear (applause from multiple audiences affirming it)*
- *I feel (excited, happy and more confident that it's a top seller)*

After selecting a book topic that stands out in the crowd and sells, develop a way of making your book different. You need a different viewpoint, a niche, or a different spin on perhaps the same information. Examine the problem again. Look at the solution your book solves with the goal of coming up with a way to present your knowledge differently than existing books.

TAP INTO THE BOOK WRITER INSIDE YOU

Have you given up on writing your book? Don't give up! Others have taken their dream off the shelf this year. You can too! First, let's get rid of the top two book writer blocks. You don't like to write that much and think you have to hire a ghost-writer. You hate research and think you have to do tons of research. The good news is you don't have to hire a ghost-writer or do tons of research.

Your readers just want solutions to their questions and challenges. If you have the answers, you can be on your way to writing an easy to read, well organized, compelling book. Don't hold back any longer; tap into your natural book writer. Your audience will love reading your book full of solutions to their challenges.

Here are some tips to help you tap into the natural book writer inside you:

1. **List top questions and topics of your audience.** For instance, if you want to write a book to help those in your work field, what questions do you hear the most in your daily work? What concerns and topics always come up in your area of expertise? In a book about dieting versus life style eating changes, my dietician friend asked questions like: where are you now in dieting? Why do you go from diet to diet with little success? What are your weight goals? Her topics included 7 solutions through life style eating changes and exercise.
2. **Write the number one challenge your book will solve.** Successful book writers focus on one topic per book. Each chapter of information must support this number one challenge. Again, my dietician friend's audience number one challenge was how to lose weight naturally through lifestyle change eating and exercise without pills, surgeries, etc. All of her chapters are solutions supporting that one goal.

3. **Develop a working title.** Speak to your audience in this title. In a few words let them know how your book will help them. "Lose Weight Naturally in 7 Easy Steps" could have been a working title for my dietician friend. Even if this working title is not quite the one you end up with. It will serve to help keep you inspired and your writing focused. Focused writing becomes a compelling book. If your writing becomes scattered and unfocused your reader's attention may scatter as well. If you lose their attention, they may never finish your book.
4. **Group your top questions and topics into categories.** Your categories are actually your chapters. Give each category/chapter a working title. When you start writing the solutions to each chapter, you don't have to start with chapter one. Start with whatever topic you feel passion bubbling at the moment. Better yet, start with the easiest to build momentum. Load benefits into your chapter titles.
5. **Write your chapter introduction.** The introduction should include a hook and a short statement about why your audience will read the chapter (thesis statement). The hook need only be 1-2 sentences like a powerful quote or 2-3 questions that lead the reader into the content. Though short, your thesis statement should include benefits. Remember keep answering the question for your reader, "What's in it for me?"
6. **Assign one question per chapter.** Focus on one question or challenge in each chapter. After asking the question, write the solution with your tips, how-tos, inspiration and stories. This will become the bulk of your chapter. Don't forget to use engagement and interest tools like headings, sub-headings, list, pull quotes, side-bars, worksheets to keep your reader engaged and reading. A straight page of text may put your

reader to sleep. When they wake up they may never pick your book up again.

7. **Write your chapter ending.** Your non-fiction chapters should always have a summary. Give each chapter an ending of about the same length. After the ending, you can include action steps or thought prompters followed by a 1-2 sentence enticer statement leading your reader to the next chapter. Make it your mission to get your reader to want to keep reading to the next chapter. Include a couple benefits that they can look forward to in the next chapter.

If you don't use the above principles, you may be this time next year still wondering if you can make your book dream a reality. My vote says you can do it. You know the problems your audience face; now write the solution. Your audience will reward you by buying your easy to read, compelling book and telling all their friends about it. Go ahead tap into the book writer inside you and make your dream a reality.

Got an idea for your book yet?

You are SPECIAL! Please, forgive me for shouting. But, I want you to remember that? You are one in a billion-even zillion! You are a unique individual. No one has lived your life like you have and no one is more ready to advise, help or encourage other people who are facing or about to face what you have.

Ask yourself these questions:

Who am I? What am I passionate about? Am I in my twenties or fifties? Do I attend school or college, just started work, leaving work, at home with small children, rearing teenagers, retiring, starting my own business or laid off(!?!) or just travelling the country? Do I have responsibilities: to parents, brothers/ families, to adopted family, to friends, to colleagues, to a boss or job?

Even better, what challenges have I had with life and

how have I overcome them? Remember challenging or tough experiences are excellent teachers too (In fact we learn more about life and ourselves during the tough times than good experiences.) Perhaps you have experiences you can share in a non-fiction book because you've:

• been ripped off in the mortgage crisis • lost a lot of money on an investment • survived bullies at school • found an easy way to get great grades • just completed your tax return yourself • overcome the loss of a close family member	• visited the Grand Canyon • raised $xxxxxx for your favorite cause • found a great job during an economic downturn • bought a house in a recession. • found a really great job period. • found a way to lose weight safely & keep it off

...each of these experience is worth a whole lot to someone who is about to experience them. And as you've lived through it, you will be able to explain and relate the whole thing like nobody else. Let's look at a quick example of what a "non-fiction" book might look like...

Example: The New Thirty at Forty: Fit at Forty & Beyond

Let's put on our thinking caps and suppose that your target audience is in their forties with an emphasis on forty. What could you do in order to select a topic?

You could create a book designed around, "Getting Fit at Forty" like the example I gave earlier. In each chapter you might share what kind of diet and exercise involved in getting fit at middle age, the challenges one might have, helpful hints for various aspects of middle age, etc.

What's great about this particular idea is that you can then create a "The New Forty at Fifty" and write a sequel or a series of books for fitness at each stage of life!

Are you getting excited yet? Anyone can write a non-fiction book! We all have experiences including challenges and victories that others would find valuable and could learn from such as:

1. Getting Married
2. Having a Baby
3. Bringing Up Children
4. Living With Teenagers
5. Dealing With Bereavement
6. Being A Student
7. Shopping for Bargains
8. Coping With Divorce
9. Buying/Selling a House
10. Making Your Own Designer Clothes
11. Designing a Garden
12. Getting a Job
13. Starting Your Own Business

14. Managing Staff
15. Managing Your Time
16. Investing Your Money
17. Study skills for students
18. Improve your memory
19. How to work your way through college

I literally could go on and on - there are thousands of possibilities. But, I won't; I believe you get the idea.

THIS WEEK'S ASSIGNMENT

1) Find and shape your book idea. If not already, first of all pray about what God would have you write. Ask for His guidance , wisdom and direction. Then list three skills or interests that you feel most passionate about. Which of these skills or interests would you like to discuss further in a book manuscript and why?

What are a few of the most interesting aspects of your ministry, business, favorite cause, skill or hobby? Which of these would you choose as a theme for your book and why? If you have already chosen your topic, explore your chosen topic and developing an angle or a targeted market for it. ***Alternative:*** *locate an intense problem & solve it in your book. Write the prescription for this intense problem in your book and you will sell more than you anticipated!*

2) Write a faith vision for your book. Specifically name the results you will experience (see, hear and feel) and a related scripture. Place these results (faith affirmations) along with the book title in color on a 3x5 card. Position it near your workstation or on your bathroom mirror. Put it somewhere you will see it daily. Use the current date including the year: Now that my book (title and subtitle) is finished and is a huge seller. For example:

- *I see (smiling people at my speaking engagements buying it) or (hundreds of orders from my web site)*
- *I hear (applause from multiple audiences affirming it)*
- *I feel (excited, happy and more confident that it's a top seller)*

____

____

____

3) Over the next few days, pull out all of the existing information related to your book topic. Begin to organize this information into topics. Write below at least 3 groups of information that you will pull from. i.e. career, hobby, research.

____

____

____

4) Organize all of the information you pulled out. Include the notes you jotted down for your book. Start below your list of topics you found.

____

____

____

Special Invitation: For extra guidance and support. I invite you to sign-up for the *Book Writing Course* 12 week online course (membership site) for bonus reports and free coaching including *The Magic of the 100 Day Timeline* http://www.bookwritingcourse.com/specialoffer.htm

WORDS WORTH REMEMBERING:

Thoughts and ideas are the source of all wealth, success, material gain, all great discoveries, inventions and achievement.
—Mark Victor Hansen

Coming Up Next ...

Chapter #3:
Pillar 2: Planning – Map Your Book Journey With a Plan"
In the next lesson we'll cover **planning.** In the "planning" stage you will discover the difference between your *book marketing plan* and your *book proposal*. You will in essence create a map for your book journey.

CHAPTER 3

Mapping Your Book Journey With A Plan

Write the vision, and make it plain upon tables;
that he may run with it who reads it.
—Habakkuk 2:2

I mentioned in last week's lesson, writing a successful book involves *four pillars.* Last week we examined pillar #1, which was **Preparation**. In today's lesson we'll examine the second of the four pillars of a successful book pillar #2: **Planning**. Today we start planning your book.

For the purposes of this course, Your WIN is the successful completion of your book marketed to a targeted audience with more book sales than you dreamed. Your map is a written marketing plan including the goal, the route and passion points (signs) along the way. The book writing course is your vehicle of choice to take you to your goal.

Starting your journey with a written marketing plan will guide you on your book path with ease and direction. Additionally, authors who enjoy the greatest success work from a plan even a program that begins with a book. Meaning, the book is the beginning not the end. The *Book Writing Course* program helps you describe your book, the characteristics of its market including who and why they will buy it.

Developing your book following the program explains how you will build upon the credibility and visibility your book creates. Your plan will describe how you will promote your book as well as develop multiple streams of income from it.

Following this plan, encourages you to view your book as an expandable "concept" instead of just one title. It will encourage you to build a structure and insert modules of your existing information into it resulting in easy, step by step writing of a successful book(s).

Begin by asking some fundamental marketing questions: Who is your target audience, who do you want to buy your book, what problems do they face, what motivates them (fear, anger), why will they buy your book, what benefit will your book offer its readers, what will you do to promote your book and ways you can profit from your book's success. Now let's start drawing that map.

WRITE A BOOK USING A ROADMAP TO SUCCESS

Everyday someone hops a train to start writing a book. Unfortunately as one person gets on the train to write a book there are several people who decide that it's hopeless, they'll never complete their book and get off the train.

My hope is that you will be the one who starts the journey of writing a book and stays on to completion. Staying on track to write a book is not without effort and diligence; even so you can do it with an easy road map (a system.) If you're reading this lesson, I'm almost certain you'll have to change your priorities, the times that you write and the amount that you write.

This is why writing a book is so difficult for some because it requires you to change your priorities. Or at the least move your book writing project to one of the top 3 priorities in your day.

Most of us, don't want to change, we put our goal of writing a book at the bottom of our list and think voila, and someday soon

I'll have a book! In reality, doing it this way could take years before we reach our goal.

The people who get off the train of writing a book are most likely the ones who didn't use a roadmap for success. They did not sit down and create a book writing plan. You must have a plan for your book writing; if you don't then there's no point in starting. You might be on a program that brings you close to finishing your book but because you didn't have a plan or a practical goal you abandon it and say it was not working.

The road map for success in your book writing program is to have a specific, but sensible goal. Be specific about your book writing goal. Do not tell yourself that you would like to write a book by the end of this year. That is not a specific goal. You have not set a start date, you have not set an end date and you have not stated what book you would like to write.

A specific book writing goal is stating that you are going to start your book writing program on January 28th at 5:00 a.m. during which time you want to complete your 156-page book '10 Ways to Stop Divorce Before It's Too Late' and it will end at midnight on June 30. Be as precise as you can. Now you have the beginning of the road map to start your book writing journey.

Your next step in this plan is to be practical. Your goals have to consist of a goal that can be achieved. If you state that you would like to write a book in the next few weeks working a couple of hours a week, you are setting yourself up for failure. Not only will you not achieve this goal but also it will cause you to possibly give up because your plan was unrealistic.

Start your book writing plan with a goal that you know you will be able to achieve if you just challenge yourself to achieve. Writing a book in 12 weeks working at least 20 hours a week is something you can do and you will not have to say good-bye to your family and become a hermit to achieve it.

Don't wait any longer; begin your book writing journey with

a road map. Start seeing yourself writing and completing a book by your end date (100 days.) Before you know it, you'll have a finished book in your hands all because you started with a road map to guide you to the finish line. Here are a few more tips to mapping your book journey with a plan.

When writing my first book, a writing mentor and friend of mine said, "I heard you were writing a book. That's great. Do you have a map yet?" Of course being new to writing books, my question was, "What's a map?"

A map would have been my plan and my intent to write a book including my table of contents. Since then my map (plan) includes a lot more. Which is what I will share with you in this chapter though it includes a lot more; it will definitely be in the same simple form and language. I still like simple, straightforward language, don't you?

Look at it this way; you have more to gain than anyone in the success of your book. Therefore, when mapping your book journey you should:

1. **Set realistic expectations.**
I hate to be the one to break the news to you. But I felt I must be honest. Many writers set themselves up for failure by having wrong expectations. The reason successful authors and writers embrace a plan (program) is because they know it is highly unlikely they will get rich from sales of their book.

They know writing and publishing a book will change their life. But they realize that most of the rewards will come from sources other than their publisher. You must realize your book is a product and as a product it has to be marketed. Your plan provides a map for everything you do afterwards.

Know the difference from your book plan and proposal

Your book marketing plan is what I describe as your map. It describes your book, what you will do after the book is completed and published. It also describes who you hope to sell your book to – target audience. For more information on writing a successful book marketing plan see lesson 5 "Pillar # Promotion. So in short you can say your book marketing plan is your roadmap to success and profits.

Your book proposal is a sales (direct-marketing) document with a sole purpose. I've devoted one of the bonus reports solely to preparing a book proposal. For right now, let's define its purpose. *It's single purpose is to convince a publisher that your book will earn a profit, if published.* The proposal should focus on the size and buying power of the targeted market you will attract, the problem your book solves, how your book plans to solve the problem, how different your book is from others already published on the subject and how you plan to promote your book.

If you have selected a traditional method of publishing, you can and should develop your proposal before you even write your book. It will help solidify and crystallize some of your ideas. In fact, how well you develop your proposal including a detailed table of contents or chapter outline in your proposal, the easier and faster you can get started mining your ideas, creating a structure and writing your book.

The publishing world and our society have changed. Writing and publishing your book can still change your life. But now a book is not the be-all and end-all, it is simply a tool that allows you to become a more successful business person, taking the profitable road to success and destiny.

2. **Identify your targeted book market**

Why do people buy non-fiction books? Most readers buy books to solve problems or help with fulfilling a need. For example, when I started speaking for a fee I went out and bought a couple of popular books about speaking.

Browsing in the bookstore, I was attracted to Lilyan Wilder's book "7 Steps to Fearless Speaking" I read the back cover. I noticed she could help with 7 easy steps. I skimmed the table of contents, read a few lines and immediately liked her easy to read style. It went in my purchase basket.

Because I wanted to hear from several authorities on the subject, I picked up another book by Nido R. Qubein, "How to Be a Great Communicator: In Person on Paper, and on the Podium. His style of writing was not as easy to read but it still went in my purchase basket as well.

Which brings us back to my original point; people buy non-fiction books to solve problems. To identify your targeted market, pinpoint a problem they have and the solution of course.

Problems come in all shapes and sizes. Usually a general category problem applies to all types of markets.

- **Special Interest.** Is your golf game, card game, tennis game as good as you'd like? Are you considering taking up racket ball? Want to improve your computer skills? What ever the case may be, your need to improve or change your level of performance is considered the problem.
- **Physical Fitness.** What's the first thing you do when your doctor diagnose you are diabetic and you need to lose 20 pounds? You go look for a book that will walk you through step by step to lose weight or change your eating habits to control diabetes. You turn to an expert; someone that has solved the problem to learn from their experience.
- **Mental Condition.** Are you feeling stressful about a recession? Are you noticing more unexplained physical symptoms probably related to stress? Once again, you

have a problem and you most likely look for a solution in book form. You are happy to find someone has outlined easy steps to de-stress in our society. You gladly purchase the book outlining easy ways to bullet proof your business during a recession.

- **Personal Economics.** Are you worried about the economic downturn? Perhaps, you have experienced corporate merges, lay-offs, downsizing, or retirement and lived through it? Books that present financial solutions to economic problems during shaky times are guaranteed to succeed.
- **Business Marketing.** We live in a competitive society. Consultants, coaches, solopreneurs, professionals, small business owners and managers everywhere need a growing database of customers and clients. Consequently, there's always a group of people actively looking for: how to books that offer solutions on improving their advertising copy, improving their business image or building an effective website in their field.

Each of the problem types describes a problem and the readers need for a solution. The main goal of your book promotion plan is to identify the problem your book solves for your targeted reader and then present the solution. The more intense the problem and the easier you can make your solution, the more readers will seek out your book.

Your task becomes to re-structure your knowledge into bite-size reader solutions. Appeal to the masses, by letting them know what's in it for them and how easy the solution is with your book. For example, let's consider the book title I mentioned earlier about speaking.

The title could have been: "How to Overcome Your Fear of Speaking" instead of "7 Steps to Fearless Speaking" The latter is more appealing because it alludes to only 7 steps to my solution.

3. **Examine your competition**

Your first step in researching the competition is to visit a large book store locally or go online to http://www.amazon.com and look for similar books. Additionally, visit http://www.bn.com (Barnes & Nobles Online) and http://www.borders.com. Since you have already identified the problem you want to solve with your book, be sure to include using search engines like http://www.google.com to help find articles, reports and websites devoted to the problem.

Don't depend on your memory of what you have seen. Make notes and combine your research into a single Word document. In your notes make a list, and write down the details listed below about each book or document you find:

title and author, year of publication, sales rank reader reviews, who wrote the Foreword or Introduction, number of editions or printings

Don't be intimidated if you find more than several books already written on the topic. The fact that there's existing books shows that the topic is an active one. If you decide to go the traditional route of publishing, you will find publishers are more willing to invest money in a book on a topic with a track record than one that has no obvious market.

I encourage you to buy one or two existing books just to read, noting the case studies and references they cite as well as the quality of information they provide. You should make a mental note at least of things like:

- Is the information presented in an easy to read, helpful way?
- Is the reading a pleasant chore or is it like wading through mud?

- Is the information timely and accurate?
- Do the books contain any reader engagement tools like check-list, worksheets or questions?

One of the reasons for examining your competition's books is so that you will be able to describe in detail the strengths and weaknesses of existing books in your proposal. And the better your research, the better your proposal will be. Additionally, a good reason is because it lets you know where you can aim as far as positioning. When I was in the planning stage of several of my books, I took the steps just like I told you.

I researched to see what was already in the market and was pleasantly surprised. I saw lots of books on my chosen topic but the quality was not good. Every book I read I thought to myself, "I know I can do better than this." Now my thinking was not in a negative way. It's just that I found it exciting and motivating to me that a part of my competitive edge would be quality, well-presented information.

4. **Make your book different**

Which brings me to our next tip, "Make Your Book Different." Identifying a niche is really hot in the marketing world right now and rightly so. After you have defined a problem and solution, researched your competition, you now have to develop a different approach. With all the books in the world on your topic, it's not enough to know the solution; you have to present the solution in a different way than existing books do.

You need to develop a way of making your book different. You need a different viewpoint, a niche, and a different spin on perhaps the same information. Examine the problem again and the solution your book solves with the goal of devising a way to describe and present your knowledge in a different way than existing books. Here are several ways you can do this:

- **Market segment.** You can develop a niche by focusing

on an occupation, sex, or age group, i.e. Lose 14 Pounds in 2 Weeks: A Guide for Women Above 40, Lose Weight Safely Before, During and After Pregnancy.

- **Broadening market.** Consider appealing to a broader market: Lose 14 Pounds in 14 Days: A Guide for Working Class Men & Women.
- **Focus.** Attack a big problem by emphasizing a particular tool or technique that you have experience with. For example, show how heart attack survivors can lose 14 pounds in 2 weeks by eating only fish, white meats and walking 10 miles a day.
- **Program.** I love this one. Base your solution on the way you solve a large problem by breaking it into steps, i.e. Write Your Best Book Now: An 8 Step Program for book writing.
- **Expertise.** Base your niche on your market's previous experience with a topic, i.e. The Last Business Book You'll Ever Need!
- **Goal.** Organize your existing information around benefits of achieving the goal: Free Again, Healthy Again!
- **Affinity.** Perhaps you have a relationship with a high visibility organization that has benefited from your ideas. You can reframe your knowledge by leveraging off your association: The Bank of America Financial Program or the SMU University Weight Loss Program.

You might notice in each one of the above examples of the same market, the contents of the book would probably be the same! The books would contain the same basic ideas, suggestions, tips, etc. For example, all the books about diets would probably stress the importance of eating right, choosing the right foods in right portions and daily exercise. Yet, each book presents a different viewpoint targeting a different market.

So, have no fear about approaching the same subject as existing books. Focus in on your unique ideas and viewpoint. Remember, according to the writer of Ecclesiastes, "There's nothing new under the sun." Bernice Fitz-Gibbon eloquently said, "Creativity often consists of merely turning up what is already there. Did you know that right and left shoes were only thought up only little more than a century ago."

5. **Think book series not single title**

While developing your marketing plan, keep in mind you can expand your title into a series. Develop a concept title (see chapter Sizzling Title) but identify ways you can create future books that follow up and build upon your first book. Identify ideas and steps that you will deliberately omit from your first book to gain leverage in developing follow-up projects.

This thought pattern will prevent you from over-loading your reader with information. If you put it all in one big book you may lose some of your potential audience. Develop an easy to read book that hints of more to come. If you cover your subject so completely there's nowhere else to go with it. You'll have problems developing follow-up projects.

In light of that, while developing your table of contents; you notice one of your chapters is developing into a monster-size (information-rich) chapter. This may be the one to re-examine and deliberately remove some of the points to place in a follow-up book.

Publishers like series. Series create brands that build upon and pre-sells future books. Readers enjoy series, as well. So plan ahead. Don't try to cram it all in one book. In fact, leave room to grow and develop a follow-up project.

6. **Develop your table of contents**

Seasoned writers may do this but especially new book writers I think should begin this way. It helps you gain focus and write much quicker later on. After identifying your targeted market and streamlining your market to a niche, you should develop your table of contents and supporting ideas.

The easiest way is to take a list of problems/solutions or questions/answers that your book solve and list them as chapters. For example, here's the original outline or table of contents I started with for the *Write Your Best Book Now* book:

List of How Tos & Articles

1. *Discover 8 Secrets of Writers Who Win*
2. *9 Step Program to Profit from Your Passion*
3. *Top Ten Ways to Make Your Book Show You the Money*
4. *10 Steps to Map Your Journey*
5. *10 Top Tips to Sizzle Your Title*
6. *Mine the Gold Called Your Knowledge*
7. *How to Build a Successful House for Each Chapter*
8. *Nine Easy Steps to Speed Writing*
9. *How to Fish in the Profit Streams Created by Your Book*

Each time I completed a chapter and the points I planned to cover, I would highlight the chapter name to show my progress. It was encouraging to see the progress begin to show each time I highlighted a chapter as finished. My momentum grew leaps and bounds each time I opened up a chapter and the major points I needed to cover were already in place.

I also took to carrying my table of contents and unfinished chapter outline (supporting points) with me. Then when I had idle time at the doctor's office or on my lunch break, I would pull it out and jot down notes that popped up. For example, from the original table of contents this chapter and supporting ideas began like this:

Chapter Five: Write Destined to Win

7 Steps to Map Your Journey

Our goals can only be reached through a vehicle of a plan, in which we must fervently believe, and upon which we must vigorously act. There is no other route to success." --Stephen A. Brennan

Winner Notes:

- Know the Difference from Proposal & Marketing Plan
- Target your market
- ~~Get to know your competition~~
- Streamline your market to a niche
- Develop Your Table of Contents & Supporting Points
- Stretch your comfort zone to create a promotion plan

By examining the table of contents earlier and the chapter title and supporting ideas, you can see during the writing process some ideas and eliminated or rewritten. I ended up reorganizing this chapter but the original list is what got me started and developed momentum. So remember to take your own list of problem and solutions to develop your table of contents and supporting ideas to drive your book to success.

THIS WEEK'S ASSIGNMENT

1) Identify your book audience, purpose and core message by answering these fundamental questions about your book. (These answers will also fit right into the 1 page book proposal in a later lesson.)

1) What is your book's main topic?

____

____

____

2) What's the purpose in writing your book? Consider what motivates them, fear, anger, lack of money, etc. (Write 1-2 sentence thesis.)

____

____

____

3) Who's going to buy and read your book? What problems do they face?

____

____

____

4) What benefits will your book offer? (Name at least three.)

____

____

____

5) Write a 1st draft table of contents. (list of questions, a list of topics, etc.)

4) Do a comparative (competitive) analysis of two other books already on the market and your proposed book idea. In your analysis, do mini-studies of the chosen books on your topic including details: how many books did you find on topic, how they compare to your chosen topic, what elements were included in the books, how will your book be different and of course better?

What is your unique selling proposition? What personal benefits does your book offer its readers? *(Complete carefully; you will need this to complete your 1 page book proposal if you are using this book as a companion to the online book writing course or plan to shop for a traditional publisher.)*

Personalized coaching positions are available at http://www.bookwritingcourse.com/roundtable.htm (If nothing else, you might consider investing in the first couple of months.)

WORDS WORTH REMEMBERING:

Our goals can only be reached through a vehicle of a plan, in which we must fervently believe, and upon which we must vigorously act. There is no other route to success."
—Stephen A. Brennan

Coming Up Next ...

Chapter #4:

Jumpstart 3 - Designing Passion Points to Sell Way More Books
In the next lesson, we cover the "passion point" pillar. You will discover how to make sure each passion (selling) point of your book is designed to sell. At each selling point your potential readers encounter, he or she is usually making a decision about your book whether it's to buy it or keep reading. You will discover how to compel them to buy or keep reading your book to the end.

CHAPTER 4

Designing Your Passion Points To Sell Way More Books

Your enthusiasm has stirred most of them to action.
—2 Corinthians 9:2b

Whew! We covered a LOT of material last week, didn't we? Even so, there's still a lot to share for this week, but the assignment won't be as involved next week, so you can breathe a little...

I'm excited about this week's material because I don't see this being taught a lot. When it comes to placing strategic selling points in your book before you write it, many book coaches don't zero in on this part.

So when you finish up this lesson, you should have your back cover promo, introduction, 30 second commercial, thesis statement all done and on your way to getting a couple of testimonials.

If you've been able to keep your commitment and do your assignments week by week during our "foundational" lessons, your book project should be coming along nicely.

We've covered Pillar #1, *Preparation* and Pillar #2 *Planning*. In today's lesson we'll examine the third of the four pillars of a successful book... Pillar #3: **Passion Points**. You will discover strategic selling points to put in your book before you write it.

IMPLEMENT THE 21 PASSION POINTS BELOW, BEFORE YOU WRITE CHAPTER 1 TO SELL MORE BOOKS

Are you ready for a change your life kind of experience? Yes. Then write and publish the book you've been dreaming about. Few things hold the potential for a life changing experience like writing and publishing a book.

You can receive life long income from writing and publishing your own book. You can affect the lives of hundreds even thousands for the good. You gain the added respect of your friends and colleagues after writing your book. You can leverage the increase of fees exponentially in your business.

Even so, many new authors don't receive the rewards they deserve. They forfeit their advantages by not focusing on the strategic selling points of any book.

Put passion, but most of all marketing, into your cover title, each chapter title, each chapter's questions you will answer, rough draft of book's back cover (sales letter), the mini-billboard (elevator speech), target audience, thesis, and table of contents. You can implement these before you write a single chapter.

In fact, every part of your book should be a compelling part of your message. Every part should be written passionately and designed to be a sales tool. Touch your readers' emotion with passion for your topic and enjoy the rich rewards of a top selling book author:

Passion Point #1 Write your book's thesis statement

Write your book's central thought or main point into a one sentence thesis. This one sentence thesis proclaims the general mission of your book. It will help crystallize your message.

If you want your readers to keep reading to the end, write

tightly focused copy. Make every sentence and every chapter support your thesis statement. Better yet, if you're writing your book fast (Write Your Best Book Now – Book Writing Program) using the question-answer method the thesis is the main solution your book offers.

Passion Point #2 Write to help one specific audience.

It's true not everyone is interested in your book. But I'm convinced there's a community of people in your field waiting for you to solve their problem. What problems does your message solve for them? Develop an audience profile (picture) and keep it in front of you as you write.

That way you can visualize a real person to solve problems for. Though women buy 78% of all trade books, choosing an audience of women is not narrow enough. Chicken Soup for Mothers, Chicken Soup for the Teenager, Chicken Soup for the Prisoner and other specific groups sold way more copies than the original Chicken Soup.

Passion Point #2 Sizzle your book title.

Your title may well be 90% of the magnetic pulling power for your book. Researchers say you have 4 seconds to hook your potential buyer. An excellent title is short. The top titles are benefit driven. Don't forget to heat them up with emotion. Use terms your audience can relate to. Use action words and verbs.

Quantify change with ways and time limits. Use one or two word ideas to tell a story. Pledge change. Spark interest. Instead of "How to Write an E-book," an author friend chose the title "Ten Secrets to Write Your E-book Like a Winner." She quantified change, sparked interest and branded her title.

Passion Point #3 Pizzazz your book cover

Have you seen the sign, "We Buy Ugly Houses!" Based on the company's popularity, it works for them. But it doesn't work in the book business. Ugly book covers get overlooked. Well designed book covers sell!

75% of 300 booksellers reviewed (half from independent bookstores and half from chains) recognized the look and design of the book cover as the most important part. They agreed the jacket is prime real estate for promoting a book. On that note, your book cover design has great importance. It can cause your book marketing campaign to fail or succeed. So, I encourage you to invest in your book cover.

Passion Point #4 Develop one central thought per book.

Focus on one topic in your book. It's a known fact bestsellers focus on one main topic. Focus on one topic, and then write each chapter to support that subject.

When you overload your reader with information, you come across as disorganized, wordy and flat. Instead of including everything you know, stick to one how-to subject and include plenty of simple details with examples to make it useful to your reader.

Passion Point #5 Make it unique.

Make it special, and make it your own. Remember the acronym and term 'your USP or Unique Selling Proposition' that most marketers teach and swear by. That's as it should be but a little twist on that for your book, "Make your message stand out with your own unique selling point."

Don't copy. You can still use your successful mentor's work as a guideline but come up with your own take on a common subject.

For example, in the book "Write Your Best Book Now" the author threads some form of "win" throughout her materials. Ever heard of the Chicken Soup for the Soul series? The title changes in its audience but the Chicken Soup brand stays the same. For example, there's a Chicken Soup for Teen-agers, Chicken Soup for Mothers, and so on.

Passion Point #6 Make it your brand

Brand yourself, your business and your book. Think about the greatest benefit that you offer through your book or service. Consider your book and chapter titles. Now think about your keywords and headings on your website. Do you see a repeating word that stands out? Remember, branding can work for you too. Many think branding is for the big guys only. Don't be afraid to create your unique brand. Make it different, make it yours, make it count.

Passion Point #7 Write the back cover before you write your book.

This is ranked the second most important "Passion Point" and therefore is prime real estate for your book. Think about it in choosing a book to read for yourself, how many times has the title hooked your interest enough to pick it up? Then usually you turn it over to see if you really want to read it. On the back cover, you put the most compelling ad copy, benefits, testimonials, and a small blurb (bio) about yourself. If your prospective buyer likes it, they will buy instantly. If they need more information to make the decision, they will preview your introduction and table of contents. Remember the speaking help book I was looking for in my example earlier. I looked at the cover then turned the book over to read the back cover…

Passion Point#8 Design a 30 second "commercial for your book."

Sprinkle this commercial throughout your book, your speeches, elevator conversation, radio spots. Let your passion for your topic shine through in this commercial. After all, you only have a few seconds to make an impression on the media, the agent, the bookseller, the individual buyer. Include your title, a few benefits, and the audience. Write this commercial with sound bites that capture attention. Don't be afraid to compare your book with a successful one. i.e. the writer's "Women With Passion, Purpose & Power" is the "Purpose Driven Life" for women.

Passion Point #09 Develop your book introduction.

State the problem your reader has, why you wrote the book, and its purpose. In a few paragraphs include specific benefits and explain your format (how you will present it.) Make sure it's one page or less. Your sales message will be more subtle here. Nevertheless pinpoint and emphasize the benefits to your reader for you may still be convincing them your book is the book to buy.

"Make use of that title writing skill you acquired when developing the title of your book. Now you must give attention grabbing power to your chapter titles, headings and even bullet points for them all (if designed correctly) reach out to the skimmers and potential readers of your book flipping through deciding to read or not."

Passion Point #10 Make a table of contents.

Each chapter should have a sizzling title. If the chapter titles are not obvious, then annotate them. Add some benefits or a subtitle explaining. In "Women's Passion, Purpose & Power," the author put the word "women" in each title. Which creates more synergy, "Your Image, Your Worth, Your Name" in the titles or "A Woman's Image," "A Woman's Worth," "A Woman's Name."

Passion Point #11 Sizzle chapter titles, headings and bullet list.

Make use of that title writing skill you acquired when developing the title of your book. Now you must give attention to your chapter titles, headings and even bullet points for them all (if designed correctly) reach out to the skimmers and potential readers of your book flipping through deciding whether to read or not.

If done right, headings and chapter titles will pull your audience in for the read or simply keep them going to complete your book. To get more readers and ultimately more sales of your book, sizzle all points of your book that have the potential to capture attention and lead your readers in for more.

Passion Point #12 Get Testimonies for your book.

After an initial contact of asking for feedback, resend them the same chapter and the table of contents of your book. Then, ask for a testimonial. These experienced contacts' testimonials will lend influence to your back cover making it a powerful sales tool.

Passion Point #13 Create a mini-website for your book.

Look for ways to engage and involve a nurturing relationship with readers and peers. Creating a website for your book is a passion perfect place to get started connecting with your potential readers and existing fans. You should seek to include the support of your family, friends, readers, other authors, book coaches and others who feed your enthusiasm. Most are eager to provide ideas, assistance and feedback.

Passion Point #14 Write a sales letter for your book.

Keep it simple. Write your targeted audience a letter about how your book will help them. Tell them why you wrote your book. Let them know who read it and loved it. Your sales letter will become your mini-salesman who sells your book 24/7.

Passion Point #15 Make your book brief.

Give yourself a break. You don't have to write a 350 page book like your colleague to be successful. It doesn't even have to be 150 pages. Simply write a short book approximately 10-100 pages long and fill it with your insightful information, your expertise and/or your experiences.

Passion Point #16 Write your book the easy way.

Write the solution. Identify 8-10 questions or problems for each chapter. Speed your writing time by simply writing the answers to each problem or question. Include your stories and experiences to add interest to your book.

Passion Point #17 Write your book vision intention.

Oprah Winfrey says, "Writing your intentions down and watching them manifest is one of the most powerful goal setting experiences ever." Write the date your book will be published and the specific outcomes.

For example, write down what you will hear, see, and feel now that the book is finished and people are reading it. You'll find it's much easier to envision a finished outcome than it is to keep hoping it might happen.

Passion Point #18 Plan to market your book the easy way.

Create a book marketing plan or revise your old one to include Internet marketing. Your book marketing plan is what I often describe as your map. It describes your book, what you will do after the book is completed and published. It also describes who you hope to sell your book to target audience.

Passion Point # 19 Think Series

Enlarge your vision. Top selling authors focus on a series of books rather than one book. Publishers look for concepts that can be expanded into a series of books rather than individual titles. Even your readers (if they like it) will look for the sequel.

Passion Point #20 Invest in educating yourself about book writing.

If you don't know how to write a book fast, enroll in a book writing mini-course, join a book writing group or purchase a book about writing books. Are you on a shoe-string budget? Subscribe to a book coach's newsletter and receive articles and book writing tips. Or considering visiting the website http://www.100DaysToABook.com for 30 days of inspiration and bite sized tips to jumpstart your writing or go along with a friendly mentor.

Passion Point #21 Get your book to market sooner.

Include your book in your top priorities. If it doesn't make it into your top plans, it may take years to complete. Set a plan in place including when you write, how much you write and even when you will finish. Make your book a top priority at least 5 days a week; get to market faster and profit sooner.

No matter how good your book is, if you don't use the passion points above in the makeup of your book you may never sell as many books as your message deserves. Infusing every part of your book with passion will create a powerful sales tool, thereby hooking and stirring your potential customers to buy a book for themselves and their friends.

Remember, if you need extra instruction, go sign-up for the *Book Writing Course* membership site to download extra Passion Point bonus reports including *How to Seal the Sale with Your Book Introduction and Table of Contents* http://www.bookwritingcourse.com/specialoffer.htm

THIS WEEK'S ASSIGNMENT

1) Action Step: Pull out a sheet of paper or write below; number 1-9. List at least 9 passion points for your book.

____

____

____

2) Review an example of the back cover for 3 separate non-fiction books. (Examine the back cover title, benefit summary, bio and testimonies if they have them and write your findings below.)

____

____

____

3) Write first draft book introduction. Tell your book reader why you wrote the book, what to expect while reading. Remember this is a selling point; so continue to convince and persuade your reader. (Need help writing an introduction? Look for part 2 of this lesson coming in 24 to 48 hours.)

____

____

____

4) Develop your 30 second commercial Include your title, a few benefits, and the audience. Write this commercial with sound bites that capture attention. Don't be afraid to compare your book with a successful one. i.e. the writer's "Women With

Passion, Purpose & Power" is the "Purpose Driven Life" for women.

5) **Re-write your book's thesis** below. Again, what's the purpose in writing your book? (Write 1-2 sentence thesis.)

6) **Write YOUR back cover sales pitch.** (Back cover title, benefit summary, bio and testimonies if available)

7) **Write your book's vision or intention statement on a 3x5 card.** Write the date your book will be published and the specific outcomes. For example, write down what you will hear, see, and feel now that the book is finished and people are reading it. You'll find it's much easier to envision a finished outcome than it is to keep hoping it might happen.

8) **What specific audience are you writing your book? Compile a profile with as much detail as possible.** Develop an audience profile (picture) and keep it in front of you as you write. This way you can visualize a real person to solve problems for. If you're finding this a little hard, picture a friend that you know likes your writing or topic and write to this person. For example, I have a special writer friend that I write all my articles to. It gives me a more personable tone. I hear all the time from readers; it felt like you were speaking directly to me.

____

____

____

WORDS WORTH REMEMBERING:

Love. Fall in love and stay in love. Write only what you love, and love what you write. The key word is love. You have to get up in the morning and write something you love, something to live for.

—Ray Bradbury

Coming Up Next ...

Chapter 4: *Develop a Promotion Plan Before You Write Ch. 1*
In the next lesson, we'll cover the **promotion** stage where you plan how you are going to get the word out about your new book and attract your initial readers, as well as developing an ongoing marketing presence to continually funnel new sales and profits on your book journey.

CHAPTER 5

Developing A Promotion Plan Before You Write Chapter 1

...Faith by itself, if it is not accompanied by action is dead.

—James 2:17

Are you an extrovert or introvert? According to which you are you may dislike the word *book marketing or book promotion*. Many introverts don't like communicating with people that much, so my introvert friends tell me how much they hate book promotion.

But the truth is extrovert or introvert, after writing your book you must let others know about it. Which is a simplistic way of saying you must promote your book to sell it. I've talked with you about putting passion points (selling points) in your book before you write it to sell way more.

But, there's one other pillar and element to writing a saleable book to success and that's planning how you'll promote your book. In these lessons, I give you some things to think about implementing in your book marketing plan. And, yes even before you write it.

Again, we cover this week's lesson in two very distinct parts

.. **Part 1: Pillar #4 (Promotion Plan)**
.. **Part 2: Book Marketing Checklist**

We've covered Pillar #1, *Preparation,* Pillar #2 *Planning* and Pillar #3 *Passion Points*. In today's lesson we'll examine the final of the "Four Pillars of a Successful Book"... Pillar #4: **Promotion Plan**. I know you may be wondering why is she talking to me so much about selling my book when I've barely started planning and writing my book.

Stay with me, there is a method behind this madness. And no, I'm not trying to make you into a book selling machine. It's just that, I've learned and want to teach you how you write your book have a lot to do with how it connects with your audience. And eventually, it can determine how well it sells.

Additionally, when you prepare your 1 page book proposal a little later you will already have this information on hand.

1-1 DEVELOP A BOOK MARKETING PLAN

Have you developed your book's marketing plan yet? You know now really is better than later. There are 2 facts to realize in developing your promotion plan. Realize it should begin the day you conceive your book idea and it never ends.

The other is the more you write the better you become at it. You need to begin building name recognition in your field. In other words, you want to begin developing your public image.

No, I'm not suggesting you become a politician but I am saying you must get involved in your book's promotion. After all, you are the one that cares the most for your project. Many authors and especially small business owners/authors dread book promotion like a plague.

They say, "With all that I already do, I jumped the hurdle of writing and completing my book, now I have to promote it as well –nooo!" Look at it this way; you have more to gain than anyone in the success of your book.

Create your written marketing plan before you finish chapter one. This plan covers your first year's launch period and lifetime plan. One of the mega mistakes newbie authors make is that they quit marketing after the initial six month honeymoon. Be patient and prepare to market your book up to three years for optimum success.

Another biggie mistake inexperienced authors make is they wait until their book is published before they even think about marketing. Your book marketing plan could include:

- how many books you want to sell in a year,
- your 30 second commercial,
- book reviews,
- news releases,
- article marketing,
- book signings, speeches or talks about your book,
- electronic newsletters and a book web site.

Without a written plan to market your book, you may miss the mark of top sales. Additionally, your book marketing plan should include:

- **Media.** Magazines, newsletters and newspapers which you can submit to for free. It's o.k. to get paid, if you must but you are most importantly after the exposure of you and your book.

- **Community groups.** Expand your public image in your field. Give your book maximum exposure; offer your expertise to community groups. Unless, your credibility is already established offer to speak for free.

- **Associations.** Explore your field's associations. Many sponsor conventions and trade shows where you can speak or serve on a panel. You be known in your associations but many don't know you've recently written a book.

Develop a list of contacts. Offer them your free articles that combine your knowledge and focuses on their organization's needs.

Develop your website. If you don't have one that focuses on your book or you as an individual, create one. Your website is now one of the first places agents, publishers and clients will look to find out more about you. The better quality it is, the more it will pre-sell your book proposal or your book itself. First impressions are important. Make your website a good one that accurately reflects you as an individual.

1-2 TEN GOOD REASONS YOU NEED A WEBSITE

Did you write a helpful book designed to solve your audience's problems? Yes. If your book was significant enough to write, it deserves as much exposure as you can give it. A new survey found that 23% of readers polled have visited an author's web site, while only 18% have gone to a publisher's site. Additionally, a website is a great way to get more leads and more book customers; it's one of the fastest growing tools around to help you connect with more prospects. A website will expand your exposure; increase your sales opportunities, cut expenses and more.

Here are 10 good reasons to get an author's website:

1. Add an additional income stream.

You may have already built a respected name for yourself offline. A book website will bring you even more respect. The growing group of people who embrace the Technology Age will expect you to have a website. They will reward you by buying from you. They love the convenience and instant gratification of on-line ordering.

2. Expand your reach to the world.

When your website is made available, many people will visit from all over the world. It will open the opportunity for you to interact with people outside of your immediate area. When your subscribers and customers have good success with your products or service they will tell their friends and associates. Referrals make the best customers for they bring a higher rate of sales.

3. Build your brand name.

Enhance your prestige as a professional. Let your readers know why your product or service is the best choice. Build quality into your work so your customers will enjoy spreading the word about your product or service. As I am sure you have heard before, your customers are your best marketers.

4. Create more product awareness.

Offering free articles and tips to your website visitors will go a long way to create more awareness of your product or service. 85% of internet users are looking for information. Make it your intent to give something useful and helpful in your area of expertise. As your visitors come for the free, they will become aware of your product or service. They may not buy the first or even the fifth time but expert statistics say up to 50% will buy.

5. Follow up on your leads fast.

When you invite your readers to leave their email address through testimonials or free articles you can stay in touch with them. Offer a free chapter or excerpt from your book. Draw a picture with benefits and great testimonials why they should sign-up for your free newsletter.

You have grown your business or service; now develop your website to enjoy watching your profits soar to new heights. Stay in touch with your buyers. When they order from your website follow up with them. Start building your list and send them regular follow-up information, free bonuses and requests.

6. Grow your existing sales opportunities.

Send out and setup post cards, speeches, book signings, and radio interviews with a toll-free 800 order number for non-techies. Be sure to offer a special price on your book. Improve your customer service and support systems for many enjoy buying online and expect a smooth process. Don't disappoint your online customers.

7. Save on support costs.

Wishing for the rented office space, new equipment, new matching furniture and support staff. Keep working toward your wish. Meanwhile, use online marketing through a website to get easier, cheaper and more effective results than mail, telephone or fax.

8. Cut the cost of doing business.

Set up a home-based virtual office with much less overhead. With online marketing you spend less time and money on postage, packaging or mailing. You don't have to depend on brick and mortar bookstores who sell your book through distribution and wholesalers as your only sales channel.

If you don't already know these channels leave you with up to 80% less profit. Online bookstores may accept your e-book & print book more readily. Visit sites such as Amazon.com or BookLocker.com for full details.

9. Increase your profits 8x or more.

On industry standard book selling sites you receive around 30% royalties for print books, 50% royalties for print e-books via checks periodically through the mail. With your own website for your information product or print book, you will get to keep all the money after expenses along with the added prestige of being an expert in your field.

10. Slash your marketing time.

Email and web communications are short, fast and targeted. You remove time hogs like buying stamps and letterhead. As an added bonus with a couple of hours a week or hiring a computer assistant you can look like a Barnes and Noble reaching thousands of online buyers by investing ongoing attention and maintenance to your website.

You have grown your business or service; now develop your website to enjoy watching your profits soar to new heights. Stay in touch with your buyers. When they order from your website follow up with them. Start building your list and send them regular follow-up information, free bonuses and requests.

MORE BOOK PLANNING

During the planning stage of your book don't forget to include the passion points (discussed in previous lessons) designed to sell your book. One of those passion points is to identify and contact the influencers in your field. As early as possible, send them your book's table of contents and two sample chapters.

The two sample chapters and table of contents help prove your commitment and intention to complete your book project. Make it your biggest goal to have a "name" or a trusted authority in your field endorse your book by either providing a brief quote or testimonial for the front or back cover.

One good way of approaching an established authority is to interview them. This establishes at least a dialog with them. In the process of interviewing, at the opportune moment you can ask for a quote or even an overview/introduction for your book project.

Some might ask for a symbolic honorarium but most will be pleased to write a brief overview or testimonial for your book project because it further promotes them in their endeavors.

Beyond quotes, your book marketing plan should include a list of review copies of your book for possible mention, review in their publication or website.

1-2 IDENTIFY FOLLOW UP INCOME

This section of your promotion plan is last because it can only be fully accomplished after your book is published whether by traditional means or self-published. After your book is released, there will be new opportunities available.

Even so, we are covering the book promotion plan at this point for it will influence the way your book is developed for publishing. If you are set on pursuing traditional publishing, it will affect the way you prepare your proposal and contract.

We noted earlier in the lessons, that the majority of your book profits will come from the doors and opportunities that the book opens for you. It's what the publishing industry calls the "back end" sales that will buy your vacation in the Bahamas, not so much advances or royalties.

We'll start by identifying your profit centers and passive income sources you plan to develop from your published book. These will center on publications and services that you offer through your website. That's why it's important that your publishing contract allow you the freedom to mention your website as much as appropriate.

Follow-up income opportunities may include:

Audio Cassettes (MP3, CDs, DVDs). Don't expect to get wealthy from them. But audio cassettes (products) will permit you to gain extra mileage from your speeches.

E-Books. These are short 10-70 page books that you write and format using your word-processor software or a desktop publishing program. After formatting, you use the Acrobat program to convert them into a PDF format (Portable Document Format.)

This allows you to sell and distribute them as downloadable files from your website or as email attachments. E-books can offer detailed treatment of specific topics that were only lightly touched upon in your original print book.

Personal Services. You should set your website up to help promote and leverage the expertise you displayed by writing your book. One on one coaching and corporate consulting are two aspects to consider. If you are a minister of the gospel, you can develop and present seminars and workshops on your book's topic.

Also, you can explore the opportunity of developing a curriculum you distribute as electronic files. Or you may develop a profitable speaking career launched from the success of your book.

Workbooks. Another form of e-books, that expands on your book's topic allowing readers to relate your ideas to their specific tasks. They usually contain guided tutorials, checklists, worksheets and progress-trackers that would have slowed the pace down in your original book.

The quicker you include follow-up income opportunities in your thinking, the easier it will be to write your book in a way that promotes these opportunities. The publishing world and our society have changed.

Writing and publishing your book can still change your life. But now a book is not the be-all and end-all, it is simply a tool that allows you to become a more successful business person or minister of the gospel taking the profitable road to success and destiny.

THE BOOK MARKETING CHECKLIST

Are you ready to sell way more books than you dreamed you would? I've got good news for you! At the time of this writing there's an Information Revolution going on. There's a whole new Internet audience waiting to hear about your insightful book that solves their problem in your field. Include Internet Marketing in your promotion plan. Use a couple of these guaranteed marketing techniques and explode your book sales to a whole new level.

_____1. Create a *book marketing plan* or revise your old one to include Internet Marketing. Your book marketing plan is what I often describe as your map. It describes your book, what you will do after the book is completed and published. It also describes who you hope to sell your book to – *target audience.*

_____2. Develop an easy author's website to jumpstart your Internet marketing plan. If you don't have one that focuses on your book or you as an individual, create one. Your website is now one of the first places clients will look to find out more about you. The better quality it is, the more it will pre-sell you and your book itself. First impressions are important. Make your website a good one that accurately reflects your book and you as an individual.

_____3. Know the one sentence version of your "mission statement" to attract new targeted clients through email. Remember prospects don't buy your education or career titles, they want to know what's in it to help them. Place that one sentence as the second line of your signature file.

_____4. Put your power-packed signature file at the bottom of each email you send. It will soft-sell your book each time you contact someone via email. Be sure to develop different signature files for different promotions. Use each one to drive targeted visitors to your book's website.

_____5. Write a sales letter for each book you want to sell. Like a mini-salesman, your sales letter will sell your book 24/7 and make you money even while you sleep.

_____6. Use benefits and features throughout your marketing

copy. Do you know the difference? Knowing that benefits sell and features explain make your promotions like a magnet that attract your best customers.

_____7. Create cds, tapes and videos of your speeches promoting your book. Then package them and sell them from your website. Post mini-audio clips to offer your web visitors a sample. Additionally, you can choose a speech and offer it as a gift to your web visitors. They can listen to it On-Demand or use it as an incentive to sign-up for your ezine.

_____8. Create short articles from your book excerpts and submit to ezines, directories and online groups. The articles will help build your credibility as an expert in your field. Additionally, the signature files at the end of each article if developed correctly will drive thousands of targeted visitors to your website.

_____9. Develop and email your own ezine that helps you stay in touch with prospects to build trust. Does a newsletter sound overwhelming? Try doing a short e-column on the subject of your book. Either way make sure you follow up with your visitors. Researchers say most will buy after 5-7 exposures to your sales message.

_____10. Create a short eBook on a similar topic as your book to help brand your business and attract new readers. A short ebook of 10-100 pages could turn into a traffic virus that's contagious to all your web visitors. Soon your name would be known as one of the experts in your field.

_____11. Teach a free chat room class on a subject related to your book. You could install a chat room on your web site or use a free one from another web site. Before the class starts tell them a little about yourself..

_____12. Publish a section on your web site called "About Us" or "About Author." With your information you could also include pictures or some of your personal interest. This shows people you are not hiding behind your business.

_____13. Write an article on your area of expertise. Include a resource box at the end of the article. You can add information about yourself in the resource box. E-mail the article to web sites or e-zines that accept article submissions.

_____14. Participate in online communities like newsgroups, discussion boards, e-mail discussion lists and chat rooms. You will meet many people and in return they will enjoy getting to know the famous author you are becoming.

_____15. Offer free consulting to your web visitors. You could do it via e-mail or phone. They will get to know you and feel more comfortable buying your book.

_____16. Create and giveaway a free information product on your book website. In the freebie product include a section called "About The Author" or an "Additional Resources" section. Also, include an advertisement for your book.

_____17. Sign up on 1-3 social media websites. Facebook, Twitter, LinkIn, and Hub pages are popular right now. Make friends and let people know about your book through your profile and signature files. Be careful not to drive your new friends away by over selling them.

_____18. Create a free mini-course (5-7 lessons) on the subject of your book. Put it on auto responder and invite your web visitors to sign up. Put a small sponsorship ad for your book at the top of each lesson.

_____19. Promote yourself offline; teach a free class offline, speak at business seminars, join a business club or association. Assemble fundraisers for charity. These are just few ideas to promote yourself offline.

_____20. Donate your time, products, or services to charities. You can list the charities you've contributed to on your book's web site. This will show visitors that you care about others.

_____21. Design a mini-workbook for your book. If your topic can be formatted this way; you can use it as a companion resource. Offer as a free bonus; when someone purchases your book.

If you don't put *Internet Marketing* in your promotion plan, you could be in for a disappointing level of sales. Don't wait join the Information Revolution today; implement any of the above marketing ideas to explode your book sales to a new level. Discover the promotion techniques it takes to have an abundance of customers every month.

You don't have to be a famous copywriter to write effective sales letters. In fact, you have everything it takes to write an order-pulling sales letter for your book. You have the passion, the knowledge of your product (book) and now the sales letter template. Follow the above 8 steps to get organized and then write your compelling letter to convince every prospect that your book is the one they want.

THIS WEEK'S ASSIGNMENT

1) List 5 ways you will promote your book after it's published; include media, associations or community groups.

2) List 2 follow up income opportunities you plan to pursue after your book is published.

---

3) Write a book marketing plan. Include as much detail as possible.

WORDS WORTH REMEMBERING:

If you go to work on your goals, your goals will go to work on you.
If you go to work on your plan, your plan will go to work on you.
Whatever good things we build end up building us. –Jim Rohn

<u>Coming Up Next</u> ...

Chapter 4: *Give Your Book the Test of Significance*
In the next lesson, we'll cover one of the most asked questions about writing a book: How to know if your book will sell well before you write it.

CHAPTER 6

Giving Your Book The Gift Of Signicance

...And let us consider how we may spur one another on toward love and good works .

—Hebrews 10:24

Have you felt your message would be insignificant in an overcrowded market place? A friend of mine said, "I'll probably never write a book because there are already too many books on every subject I can think of."

The truth is many successful authors have felt their message insignificant in the LARGE scheme of things. But at some point they had to realize what I'm about to tell you, "With all the great books in the marketplace, there's only one voice that's uniquely yours. I am convinced there are people waiting for your perspective, your solution, or your message. They're waiting to be inspired, entertained or helped by YOUR book."

Later in the lesson I'll show you how to give your book the test of significance. After all, even if it's the tiniest of markets it will have to compete for proper attention in this hi-tech world? For your book to be able to compete in a world like ours today, you must target a niche market related to your book. Let me explain...see lesson below.

1-1 MAKING YOUR BOOK DIFFERENT

Have you wondered if your book could stand out in the marketplace and sell? The way to make your book stand out in a crowded market is to target a niche market related to your book's topic. Identifying a niche is really hot in the marketing world right now and rightly so. You may remember these principles from an earlier lesson. Some principles are worth repeating. Even so, I'll make sure to keep the repeating to a minimum.

Simply put, to target a niche market in your book's topic area: Identify a problem/solution and research your competition. Then develop a different approach. With all the books in the world on your topic, it's not enough to know the solution. You must present the solution in a different way than existing books do.

Develop a way of making your book different. You need a different viewpoint, a niche, or a different spin on perhaps the same information. Examine the problem again. Look at the solution your book solves with the goal of coming up with a way to present your knowledge differently than existing books. Here are seven simple ways to do this:

- **Market Segment.** You can develop a niche by focusing on an occupation, sex, or age group, i.e. Lose 14 Pounds in 2 Weeks: A Guide for Women Above 40, Lose Weight Safely Before, During & After Pregnancy.
- **Broadening Market.** Consider appealing to a broader market: Lose 14 Pounds in 14 Days: A Guide for Working Class Men & Women.
- **Focus.** Attack a big problem by emphasizing a particular tool or technique that you have experience with. For example, show how heart attack survivors can lose 14 pounds in 2 weeks by eating only fish, white meats and walking 10 miles a day.

- **Program.** I love this one. Base your solution on the way you solve a large problem by breaking it into steps, i.e. Write Your Best Book Now: An 7 Step Program for book writing.
- **Expertise.** Base your niche on your market's previous experience with a topic, i.e. The Last Business Book You'll Ever Need!
- **Goal.** Organize your existing information around benefits of achieving the goal: Free Again, Healthy Again!
- **Affinity.** Perhaps you have a relationship with a high visibility organization that has benefited from your ideas; you can reframe your knowledge by leveraging off your association: The Bank of America Financial Program or the Southern Methodist University Weight Loss Program.

You may have noticed in each one of the above examples of the same market, the contents of the book would probably be the same! The books would contain the same basic ideas, suggestions, tips, etc. For example, all the books about diets would probably stress the importance of eating right, choosing the right foods in right portions and daily exercise. Yet, each book presents a different viewpoint targeting a different market.

So BE BOLD; have no fear about approaching the same subject as existing books. Focus in on your unique ideas and viewpoint. Remember, according to the writer of Ecclesiastes, "There's nothing new under the sun." Bernice Fitz–Gibbon said so eloquently, "Creativity often consists of merely turning up what is already there. Did you know that right and left shoes were only thought up only little more than a century ago." Now go start your successful book journey. Make it different. Make it count. Make it yours.

2-2 GIVING YOUR BOOK THE 21 POINT TEST OF SIGNIFICANCE

Are you ready to test your book's significance? Many hopeful authors tremble in their tracks wondering if their book will sell. That's a good question. Who wants to invest time or money into a sinking ship? Don't be afraid; here's how to test your book's significance.

You can know your book is significant if it presents useful information, answers important reader questions, and impacts people for the good. If it's entertaining or funny it could go further than you imagined.

It's significant, if it creates a deeper understanding of animals, humanity or this world. With one to three of these elements your book is worth writing. More than three, it has potential of making great sales even to best seller status. If your book proves significant then it is saleable.

Here are a few tips to help you know if your book will sell well before you even write it. Give your manuscript the test of significance. Now, get started; write your book and make the world a better place.

____ **Does your book help your readers gain a new skill?** Thousands of people search for specific information daily. They want simple to read and easy to understand information. Seek to educate your audience; include engagement tools in your book. They may want to learn how to change their car oil or build a deck. Educate your audience and your book becomes significant.

____ **Does your book solve a vexing problem for your audience?** Get this right and you could have a best seller. Do you know the solution to a vexing problem? Write the solution in your book. You might be surprised at who's searching for a little relief from a stressful problem. Remember, problems come in all sizes, shapes and categories.

____ **Does your book offer expert advice, inspiration, hope to a specific group of people?** Target a group of people within your broad market. Your target group could be single dads, moms or working moms. For example, the Chicken Soup series for Teen-Agers, Mothers, even Prisoners sold much better that the original more general Chicken Soup for the Soul.

____ **Does your book offer an opportunity to learn something new or interesting?** Sprinkle your book with little know interesting facts about your topic. Be careful to avoid information overload with pages of detailed statistics. But if you sprinkle them as morsels throughout your book, you create anticipation that will lead your readers through to the end. People love statistics and bite-sized trivia about just about any topic.

____ **Does your book offer an easy to read style to learn about something?** Take a complex subject in your field and make it simple. Most people enjoy an easy reading language. The Dummies series catapulted this concept to new heights with all kinds of complex subjects made simple. Your readers will not only reward you by reading to the end but they will be happy to tell all their friends about your insightful easy to read book.

____ **Does your book offer original, different information?** Have you wondered what makes a new diet book sell well even when there are scores of diet books on the market? The author presents their unique set of successful diet rules, their exercise program, their perspective, their testimonials and their credentials. They use original, different information for the same results.

____ **Will your book inspire people to do something good?** Weave inspiring stories into your book and sell more. The *21 Irrefutable Laws of Leadership* spent 18 straight months on the Business Week Business Best Seller List. Dr. Maxwell started each chapter with a short story of a famous person successfully using the chapter's law of leadership.

____ **Is your book funny or entertaining?** Do you have a talent to make people laugh? Use it in your book. Provide a little oasis of escape for your readers. People love it when you entertain them. In fact, it's one of two basic reasons people read anything.

Intertwine funny stories into your non-fiction manuscript. Seek to entertain your audience, make them laugh; they'll love you for it. Best of all, they will have fun telling all their friends about your funny book. (Later in the course, I'll give you some important tips to build entertainment into your chapters.)

____ **Does your book offer greater understanding of life?** Have you been gifted with a deep wisdom about life? Put small excerpts of your understanding throughout your book. Sprinkle your quotes along with other famous philosophers or world thinkers within your book. If you have special understanding of human nature, bless the global community with it in your book.

____ **Does your book offer a greater understanding of nature?** Are you passionate about nature and its beauty? Perhaps you want to make strides in preserving our planet Earth. Write about it in your new book and share it with the world. Who knows you may move a whole generation. The Baby Boomer generation is talking about Jacques Cousteau books, inventions and documentary films of the ocean.

____ **Does your book present great perception of animals?** For instance, if you have a deep understanding of animals the animal lovers will lap your book information up. (smile) Write a book and fill it with your special understanding of animals. Express your passion well and you could be next Horse Whisperer Monty Roberts or Dog Whisperer Celan Milan.

____ **Does your book offer success experiences that motivate your audience to do more, give more or share more?** Share your experiences to motivate your audience. Share how you overcame seemingly insurmountable challenges in your life or professional field. It will motivate your audience to think if you did it; they can do it too.

____ **Does your book help people save money**. They may want to invest for the future or save for a big purchase. They want to free up up cash in their budget during the recession. Or they may just be looking for a bargain. Write a book that helps others save lots of money and you may have a top seller on your hands.

____ **Does your book offer ways to save time.** Most people want to work less and spend time enjoying their family and life's pleasures. Even if you just put time-saver tips in your book, it will be more appealing to a broader audience.

____ **Does your book help others look better.** Perhaps your audience wants to lose weight, tone their body, or improve their facial features. Your content is significant if it makes them feel more attractive.

____ **Does your book help people live longer.** A new wave of people groups want to get in shape, eat better or gain extra energy. Help people live longer; your book will be significant and make them feel healthier.

____ **Does your book help others feel loved and desired**. Many don't want to be lonely anymore or want to start dating again. Show them how to re-enter the dating game. Or you could simply show them how to be single and happy. Write a book that makes them feel wanted.

____ **Does your book help others in their marriage**. There are lots of couples who don't have a clue as to how to gain a successful marriage. Do you have a special compassion for struggling couples? Write your book filled with marriage success tips and encouraging words for a marriage on the rocks.

____ **Does your book help parents raise a family**. There are no manuals passed out before parents start a family. If you have special insight to help parents raise toddlers, teenagers or anything in between, fill your new book with this information. Do it right and you could have a top seller on your hands.

____ **Does your book** help people gain friends and be popular. They may want to be a famous celebrity or be more popular in school or work. Your book will make them feel praised and admired.

____ **Does your book** assist your audience in gaining pleasure. They may want to satisfy their appetite or sexual desires. This will make them feel more fulfilled.

According to experts, of the ten significant areas your book need only have:

1 for a newspaper or magazine article
2 for a significant book
3 for a best seller
5 for a Pulitzer Prize
6 for literary classic

Are you ready to start writing yet? Did your book idea pass the test of significance in at least two areas? Great, it will sell! Now that you know your book is significant, go ahead take the plunge. Don't hesitate any longer. Your audience is waiting for your unique ideas and viewpoint. Make it different. Make it count. Make it yours.

Now that you know your book is significant, here are 21 more good reasons to write your book:

21 EXCITING REASONS TO WRITE A BOOK THIS YEAR!

Have you been dreaming of writing a book this year? According to a recent survey the *New York Times* reported, 81% of people feel that they have a book in them and should write it. Why not join the list of authors who acted on that thought?

Writing a book is a great way to position you to charge higher fees, create additional income streams and go on more vacations. A book will expand your exposure, add credibility and increase your opportunities for adventure. Still not convinced? Here are 21 more exciting reasons you should write a book now:

1. **Write a book now; for now is better than later.** Kill procrastination by acting now. Sign up for a course? Read a good book about book writing. Sketch out your book writing plan. Remember you become a successful author the minute you start moving toward your worthwhile book goal. I don't know anyone that regrets they wrote a book. But I know plenty of people that regret they didn't do it sooner.

2. **Write a book and extend your reach to the world.** When your book is ready for purchase, many people will get it from all over the world. With your extended reach, opportunities for you to interact with people outside of your local area will come. Write a good book; make it easy

for your subscribers and customers to tell their friends and associates. Remember, referrals always make the best customers and bring a higher rate of sales.

3. **Write a book and go places you've never gone.** At the least, your book will travel to countries and places you've never gone. Better yet, add speaking about your book's topic to your list of services and watch new doors and opportunities for you open. Either way, writing your book will open opportunities to go places you may not get to go any other way.
4. **Write a book and create multiple income streams.** Don't just plan a one book event but plan a series of books. It's important to expand your thinking to the possibilities after your book is published. Plan to produce articles, books and updates that help your readers and help you profit from your passion. Each new book or related material will create new profit opportunities, further enhance your visibility and reinforce your credibility as an expert.
5. **Write a book and become famous.** Grow your name to fame. Write a book filled with success experiences that motivate your audience to give more, do more or share more. Share your experiences to inspire your audience. Share how you overcame seemingly insurmountable challenges in your field. It will motivate your audience to think if you did it; they can do it too.
6. **Write a book and make your mother proud.** Intertwine stories into your non-fiction manuscript. Entertain your audience, make them laugh; they'll love you for it. Best of all, your family, your friends and your mother will be so proud to tell all their friends.

7. **Write a book and get paid higher fees.** Writing a book elevates you to expert level. You gain instant credibility just by having author behind your name? And that added credibility gives you the power to increase your fees to expert level up to 400% and more.

8. **Write a book and grow your assets.** Robert Kiyosaki author of Rich Dad Poor Dad says, "In simple terms, anything that puts money, or income, into your pocket is classified as a financial asset." When you write a top selling book that puts money in your pocket every month, you can list your book as an asset on your financial statements.

9. **Write a book and create the magic pill.** Offer solutions to your audience. Offer the magic pill with simple steps to solve a problem in your field. Every one loves it when we get simple solutions to our problems. Get this right and you could have a best seller. Do you know the solution to a vexing problem? Write the solution in your book. You might be surprised at who's searching for a little relief.

10. **Write a book and raise your self-esteem** by sharing your know-how in your field. People are looking for a friendly expert to show them how to do things faster, easier and with more profit. You know; share all the short cuts & secrets of your business you've learned along the way.

11. **Write a book and position yourself as an expert.** As an author of a book, you can become the *go to guy or gal* in your field. Pull potential book readers in with free articles and tips to help them. People are always looking for good information, a whopping 85% of Internet users are looking for information. Supply them with good

information and they will think of you (a trusted expert) when they're ready to buy.

12. **Write a book and expand your market.** After publishing your book to the world, you enter a global market. You have the ability to reach out and touch someone across the globe. After you write your book, your customers may live in your neighbourhood or across the world in another country. A book will extend your reach and profits to new markets.

13. **Write a book and create an electronic product.** Develop your book into an ebook. Technology has advanced making it easier and easier to electronically publish your own e-books. The profits from each sale on a per-unit basis can be 10X the royalties earned by your original book.

14. **Write a book and develop an information empire.** Now that you've finished your book, don't stop there. You can create other products from it. Just divide it into chunks, sections and parts. Dividing your book this way will allow you to refine, repeat and repackage your information. You can keep developing your book with a website and a stream of follow-up products and even services to build your brand and your profits further.

15. **Write a book and offer a new service in your business.** You can use your new book to launch a new service in your business. Or you can simply use a book to leverage your existing services to new levels. With your book, you can consider starting a career in publishing, speaking or consulting in your field.

16. **Write a book and start speaking for a fee.** Travel the world speaking about your book's topic. Does travel

excite you? For some, it excites them to go to new cities or to a country they've never been before. Well, pack your bags! Writing your book opens the door of opportunity to go places you've never been before. Add speaking about your book's topic to your list of services and watch even more new doors and opportunities for you open.

17. **Write a book and build your credibility as a service expert.** When you write a book, you get instant credibility with your colleagues and customers. They are more willing to work with you and trust you faster with book author as one of your titles. Remember, people tend to buy more and do business with people they trust.

18. **Write a book and increase your ability to compete.** A book sets you apart from the non-author colleagues in your field. Write a book this year and receive a boost of profits from your clients because they trust you more than your non-author competitors.

19. **Write a book and create name recognition** by becoming a trusted voice in your field. After writing a book, more people will recognize you. Our societies still look up to authors. It gives you a claim to fame. Write a book filled with how-to, tips, illustrations and checklist. Share your customer success stories through case studies to inspire your audience.

20. **Rise above the rest.** If you've been looking for a way to rise above your competition, writing a book will elevate you above your competitors without a book. Do a good job with your book, promote it and it may catapult you into stardom.

21. **Write a book and boost your income** by selling books at your speeches and especially your website. If

marketed well, your book can be the beginning of a whole new income stream. After your book is written it becomes your 24 hour sales person promoting your service business everywhere it goes.

Are you ready to join the ranks of successful authors? You don't have to call your family to tell them you'll be late again today. You won't even have to pull in more people to help you work harder. I can't think of a more opportune way to change your bottom line and even your life than by writing a book. Go ahead; write a book this year and watch your profits explode like a rocket headed to the moon. Here's to seeing your name in print!

THIS WEEK'S ASSIGNMENT

1) What area is your book significant? Remember, your book should pass the test of significance with at least 2 areas.

____

____

____

2) What's different about your book than 2 competing books in your field?

____

____

____

WORDS WORTH REMEMBERING:

Every author should weigh his work and ask, "Will humanity gain any benefit from it?" —Nachman of Bratslav

Coming Up Next ...

Chapter 4: *Sizzling Book Titles Sell More Books Than Dud Titles*

In the next lesson, we'll discuss how to develop a book title that pulls in readers like a magnet to metal.

CHAPTER 7

Sizzling Titles Sell Way More Books Than Dud Titles

My tongue is as the pen of a skillful writer.
—Psalm 45:1b

Breathe in deeply, hold it…and release. Do it again. Now, I feel I can talk to you with great focus from me and you.

I know I've been shooting a lot of information at you week after week. I would love to say, that's alright, no assignment this week. But I can't. So the best I can do to ease the pressure a bit is to tell you, "Just breathe and hang in there."

We finished laying the foundation a couple of weeks ago. Today, we'll cover the importance of titling your book well. It's so important; I've given it a lesson all by itself. <u>So make sure you take the time to do the assignment.</u> In my opinion, the title of a book can almost single-handedly make or break a book. Or at least, a dud title will hinder your book's chance for success in the market.

You know if you keep going <u>you will have a competitive edge on most book writers.</u> For many authors just shoot their message out in the darkness of the world. But you are about to take aim and hit the mark of a top selling book.

You should create sizzling titles designed to hook your potential readers. One of the most important skills to develop as a marketer of your book is the skill of creating attention-grabbing titles. When you master this skill you may use it in every aspect of your writing to attract more readers, more sales, improve your cash flow and increase your profits.

You will need title writing skill for your book titles, chapter titles, sub-heading. Even bullet points will have pulling power if they are developed correctly. Your website will need passionate headings to capture the attention of your web visitors.

If you don't want your book to be lost in the sea of information streaming into your reader's consciousness each day, you must title them well. In fact, any marketing material from your 5 page sales letter or tri-fold brochure to the 2 line classified ad needs the attention grabbing power of a great headline.

Titles set the stage for your potential audience. They either will work to grab your potential reader by the collar and pull them in for the read or they don't. Top titles create excitement, anticipation and enthusiasm for more. You want your titles to express the heart and passion of your message or be 'the match' that ignites your reader's interest in reading your important message.

Develop this valuable skill and you add magnetic pulling power and punch to all your marketing documents including your front book cover and chapter titles that will get your message read.

1-1 SIZZLE YOUR BOOK TITLE!

Is your book title designed to hook your potential reader? It should; titles are one of the most important aspects of your book. Did you know that the average reader, publisher or editor only spends about 4-6 seconds looking at the front cover of any book? They spend not much longer, 15 seconds, on the back cover. That leaves an author about 20 seconds to make a good impression on a potential reader. How will your title measure up?

Does your title do its job well? I mean does it help explain what's in your book? Does it capture the interest, engage, or shock the senses of your potential reader?

Expert studies show the title may be responsible for 90% of your book's magnetic pulling power. Some even say at least half of your book's success can be attributed to its title.

A dud of a title versus a sizzler title can cause your book to plummet or soar in sales. You owe it to yourself and book's success to develop your best title. After all, the better you title the more people will reach out and grab your book to read. Develop your title to have marketing appeal for the masses.

Use these top 8 title sizzlers and sell more books than you ever dreamed.

1. **Allow reader benefits to drive your title**

A winning non-fiction title immediately communicates the benefit readers will gain after reading your book. Benefit-oriented books often use the problem-solution approach. Master (A) this skill or technique and get (B) this benefit.

Readers buy non-fiction books for a "benefit" for something that will help them, grow them, profit more, less expense, less trouble, gain more time, less stress, better relationships, better health, less drama, less trauma, more energy and vitality and less fatigue.

Napoleon Hill's "Think and Grow Rich" or Dottie Walter's "Speak and Grow Rich" both instantly communicate the benefit of reading their book. They used the benefit driven, problem solution approach: Do this and get that.

Psychological studies have proven that there are certain words that can help you connect to your potential readers and motivate them to buy from you. Here's a list of words that can help you connect...

Free	Sale	How to	Healthy
Love	Now	Discover	Guarantee
Safe	Value	Introduce	Natural
New	Fun	Easy	Fast
Benefits	Save	Your	Precious
Right	Gain	Proven	Secret
You	Money	Penetrate	Solution
Alternative	Happy	Suddenly	Magic
Security	Advice	Proud	Comfortable

Use these words to help express your book's benefits rather than its features. For example, don't say "This book has x, y, z features"...instead say "This book will save you time and money because it has proven x, y, and z."

Leave out a benefit in your title and it will not be as effective in hooking your potential reader at first sight. Title your book well to sell well. Offer a solution to your readers. Demonstrate your expertise in your area so that they will move to the next step of buying your product (book), engaging your services or at least asking for more information.

2. **Use concept and Memes to connect instantly**

One of the leading rules of developing a sizzling title is to aim for a concept, a memes, a word, or phrase that tell a story that your readers can immediately connect with and want to associate with. Names that tell a story, or express a benefit, are memes. They are words or visual images that tell a story at a glance.

As a primer to developing your own title, visit Sears or any large department store and look at the brand names of their proprietary products. The short names of these products are concepts; that tell a story in an instant. At a glance you get it; you see the mini-story.

You understand the message. Examples, include Diehard batteries, Weather-Beater paints and Craftsman tools. Each products name is a concept. Think about it, which product would you be attracted to "Diehard" or "Stop Slow". Or would you choose tools with the name "Apprentice" or "Craftsman?"

Many successful books are based on concepts or memes. For example, "A Happy Pocket Full of Money" by David Cameron tells a story of happiness and money. From the title you know this book is going to be about getting more money in your pocket.

The *Chicken Soup* series instantly brings images of comfort and being cared for. It resonated with a whole generation of Americans that have bought the book into the hundreds of thousands. The Dummies series communicate anyone can read one of these books because you don't have to know anything to get it. People automatically know the book will somehow make the complex simple to understand.

When developing your title, think of a concept, a meme, or phrase, that tell a story that your readers will instantly understand and want to be a part of. You may ask where are the benefits we just discussed were so important to include. The benefits are still a part of the meme title but a suggestive part. Your mind will fill in the benefit because it's an understood part of the story. For example:

Chicken Soup brings the comfort and care of good stories. Pocket Full of Money know how to get a pocket full of money and gain happiness. Dummies communicates you don't have to be an expert to understand the book.

Don't forget when creating your title, your possibilities are limitless. Choose a title that is flexible enough to be expanded into more than one book. Think series, including other information products that can be developed and sold from your website.

3. **Spark Interest**

Another way to develop an engaging title is to arouse your prospective reader's curiosity. Tease their curiosity and they will pick it up then buy it to find out what it's about. The infamous "Who Move My Cheese: An amazing way to deal with change in your work and in your life" by Spencer Johnson had a curious title that moved millions to buy.

It stayed on the best seller list for 5+ years selling more than 14 million copies in 40 different languages. If the same book had been titled something like, "How to Deal with Change in Your Work and Your Life", few people would have been curious. But the Who Moved My Cheese teased readers with an invitation to read or at least pick it up.

Another curiosity title is Rich Dad, Poor Dad: What the Rich Teach Their Kids About Money – that the Poor and Middle Class Do Not! by Robert Kiyosaki and Sharon L. Lechter. The title instantly engages your curiosity with the question, "What would I know if my dad was rich?"

4. **Quantify Change and Add Time Limits**

Another characteristic to incorporate in developing your best title is to promise change. In your title spell out the change that readers can expect if they follow your book's precepts. Let them know what to expect. Use steps, ways and time limits to promise change.

You can add focus and credibility to your title by adding a time frame or quantifying change. C.J. Hayden's book "Get Clients Now!: A 28-Day Marketing Program for Professionals and Consultants" The first part of the title tells what the book is about. Adding now brings immediacy. The (28-Day) part emphasizes that the reader will get day-by-day instruction and probably enjoy results in less than a month.

The author's "Write Your Best Book Now!: An Easy 7 step writing program for Entrepreneurs and Writers" uses the same principle of adding immediacy with the word now. She also quantified change with the steps that communicates to the reader read this book and they will get their best book written in 9 easy steps. Other good examples of quantifying change are "The 7 Habits of Highly Effective People" by Stephen R. Covey and "7 Steps to Fearless Speaking" by Lilyan Wilder.

Another change oriented title is "Weigh Down: An Inspirational Way to Lose Weight, Stay Slim and Find a New You" or "How to Be a Great Communicator In Person, On Paper, and on the Podium: The Complete System for communication Effectively in Business & In Life.

Change motivating titles often begin by identifying their target market including the problem, event or characteristics the book address. In doing so, they promise an easy structure leading to the promised change. List instantly communicate easier success by changing big task into a series of smaller tasks.

5. **Employ Action Words like *ing* Verbs**

Successful non-fiction books often have 'ing' verbs in the titles. Action titles promise action and progress. They are easily pronounced and project motion. John Mason's "Conquering an Enemy Called Average" implies more action than "Conquer an Enemy Called Average." A verb with 'ing' implies process.

Each "ing" verb plays a part in communicating change and movement. As you review titles while developing your best title, take note of how many use "ing" verbs in the title or sub-titles. You might be surprised to discover most books do.

6. **Use the techniques of Alliteration.**

Alliteration happens when titles include parallel construction or repeated consonants as used in the title and sub-title. For example, in one of my inspiration titles, "WOW! Women of Worth: Creating a Life Full of Passion, Power & Purpose." The repeated consonants create a rhythm that cements the book's title in a reader's mind.

Tommy Newberry's "Success is Not an Accident! Change Your Choices, Change Your Life", the repeated consonants and the repeated word 'change' work together to emphasize the success technique.

Repeated sounds command respect. Mary Muryn and Cathy Cash Spellman's Water Magic: Healing Bath Recipes for the Body, Spirit and Soul. The parallelism of the 3 words at the end, plus the alliteration of the two "S" words at the end create a title that has tempo and rhythm.

7. **Create a Shorter Title with a Long Sub-Title.**

The smaller the number of words in a title, the more attractive the cover of your book can be. Many titles are two part titles. A short compelling title is followed with a longer title that explains.

A short title is easier to remember. It's easier to say and remember. Use concept words like "Point, Click & WOW!, Dummies, Millionaire Next Door. Set up memorable contradictions like "Smart Money" or "Big Mistakes."

Another thing to remember about concept titles is they often use common words. The Wealthy Barber, Rich Dad Poor Dad, or Chicken Soup for the Soul is all based on every day words.

The front cover of your book is your mini-billboard. For maximum impact and to attract attention minimize the number of words of your title. Put the larger size of the title in the corner. A long title needs a smaller type which limits its effectiveness. A short title permits the use of a large type size for greater impact. The subtitle can still be effective but with smaller type.

So, a short title explained by a longer sub-title leaves more room for a front cover blurb or testimonial from a noted authority in your field. Authority testimonials add legitimacy to your book. Shorter titles allow room for use of a larger visual or graphic to illustrate your topic.

8. **Think Easy Translation to Website Address.**

Don't forget to consider whether your title will make an easy transition into a website address. Avoid titles that are close to the website addresses of already successful book.

Your goal should be to write your website with keywords from your title. It would be helpful if your readers could intuitively find your website using a couple of the keywords from your title. For example, if someone wanted to look for a website on the Chicken Soup books, they could simply type in your browser http://www.chickensoup.com and voila their website comes up.

Remember the full title is not needed for the URL but just a couple of key words that will identify the site. For example, when I looked for the "Rich Dad" series I simple typed in http://www.richdad.com in browser to locate them. There was no need to go to my favorite search engine and type it in because the simple key words "rich dad" took me there. It's important to note the more words used, the easier it is for misspelling and transposed letters. So instead of http://www.richdadpoordad.com , they chose the web title and URL http://www.richdad.com.

Choosing your book's title to convert to a website address is better than choosing your name. It's easier for readers to remember the title of a book than the author's name. The link between book and website is also easier to include in promotional material if the site is an extension, or reflection or your book's title.

When developing your title, the best starting point is to visit http://www.amazon.com or http://www.bn.com and search through their health, business, and self-help and marketing sections. Note the current best-sellers in each category then look through the top ten reader recommendation lists.

You will find a broader range of titles in the reader recommended lists. Notice the eight principles we have just covered: "short," "concept," "benefit," or "curiosity" tile followed by a longer sub-title that explains. Notice how often "listing steps," "numbers," or "time range" appear in the titles.

Make a note of your favorite titles. You can simply write them on a sheet of paper. Take a break, overnight is best, and allow your sub-conscious mind to mull over what you have learned. You'll be surprised one day soon after your best title will emerge.

1-2 HOW TO BRAIN STORM TITLE IDEAS ANYWHERE

You have finished your manuscript. Or you've barely begun to write. Either way, congratulations! You've begun a worthy journey. But before you take your next step, you should craft a working title for your book. Is the title you currently have a sizzler or a dud?

Remember, your title may be 90% of the pulling power for your book. It would be worth your effort to create a sizzling title for your message. Researchers say you have about 4 seconds to hook your potential buyer.

An excellent title is short. The top titles are benefit driven. Don't forget to heat your title up with emotion. Use terms your audience can relate to. Use action words and verbs. Quantify change with ways and time limits. Use one or two word ideas to tell a story. Pledge change. Spark interest.

Instead of choosing to bore her readers with "How to Write an E-book" an author friend after brainstorming chose the title "Seven Secrets to Write Your E-book Like a Winner." She quantified change, sparked interest and branded her title.

Here are 5 common ways anyone can use to get uncommon book titles:

1. **Best Seller List** – Use the Best Seller list to brainstorm ideas for your book title. Start by looking at the Best Seller list at Barnes and Nobles or Amazon.com. When Jason Oman and Mike Litman wanted to title their book, they modeled a popular book called "Conversations with God" and came up with "Conversations with Millionaires." Their book achieved #1 on Amazon.com. Now it's your turn; go be inspired by your favorite best sellers list.

2. **Tabloids** – Have you stood in line at checkout, recently? I know I have. But did you read the tabloid cover pages or picked one up to browse while you waited? If so, then you've already experienced what I'm about to describe to you. The compelling headline on each tabloid is designed to reach out and grab your attention. We all know the tabloid magazines don't sell because they're filled with wholesome content. They sell because they've mastered the titling aspect of their papers. Next time you're reading the tabloid cover, examine the titles and begin to brainstorm titles for your book.

3. **Newspapers** – Newspaper headlines are designed to capture your attention. Model and compare your book title with the parts of a newspaper headline. Is your book title short and to the point? Will it capture the attention of your potential reader? When you're reading your next newspaper, take a look at all the headlines and

sub headlines. Notice how the journalist captured your attention or not.

4. **Magazines** – Magazine cover page article titles are my favorite example of great titles at work. Like newspapers and tabloids they must have titles that entice and pull at your interest to sell magazines. For example, which would capture your attention quicker, "7 Easy Ways to Lose Inches Off Your Waist" or "How to Lose Weight In Your Waist?" Most people are drawn to the specific results in the first title. Go get your favorite magazine and notice the article titles that captivate your attention.
5. **Memes** – Department stores are great places to visit and brainstorm using memes. Memes are words or visual images that tell a story at a glance. For example, visit Sears and look at the brand names of their proprietary products. The short names of these products are concepts; that tell a story in an instant. At a glance you get it.

   You understand the message. Examples include Diehard batteries, Weather-Beater paints and Craftsman tools. Each products name is a concept. Think about it, which product would you be attracted to "Diehard" or "Stop Slow". Many successful books are based on concepts or memes. For example, "A Happy Pocket Full of Money" by David Cameron tells a story of happiness and money. From the title you know this book is going to be about getting more money in your pocket.

No matter how good your book is, if you don't title it well you may never sell as many copies as your message deserves. Now go create a book title that stirs your book reader's interest to read.

Develop this valuable skill and you add magnetic pulling power and punch to all your marketing documents including your front book cover and chapter titles that will get your message read. Titles set the stage for your potential audience. They either grab your potential reader by the shirt or they don't. Create your titles to be 'the match' that ignites your reader's interest in reading your important message. Title well and prosper!

Special Invitation: Go sign-up for the Book Writing Course membership site for bonus reports including the *Book Title Tutorial Plus 21 Book Title Templates* http://www.bookwritingcourse.com/specialoffer.htm

THIS WEEK'S ASSIGNMENT

1) Brain storm at least 5 rough draft titles. (Need help brain-storming? Read bonus lesson *How To Brain Storm Book Title Ideas* including 21 Title Templates on its way to your email box in 24-48 hours.)

____

____

____

2) Choose 1 title from your rough draft titles to use as working title of your book? Choose this working title or select a chapter title and its headings. Revise them until they sizzle like bacon frying in a skillet. Vegetarian? O.k., sizzle them like a Fourth of July fire works show!

____

____

____

WORDS WORTH REMEMBERING:

"The strokes of the pen need deliberation as much as the sword needs swiftness." —Julia Ward Howe

Coming Up Next ...

Chapter 8: *Mining Your Knowledge Like Gold*

The next week's lesson is designed to help you excavate (dig up) ALL the (related) knowledge and experience you already possess and use it in your book.

CHAPTER 8

Mining Your Expert Knowledge like Gold

There is nothing new under the sun.
—Ecclesiastes 1:9b

I am excited for you. Hopefully, you are seeing your path to a saleable book with a little more clarity. My desire is that you know now better than ever that *the finish line - the completion of your book* is an achievable goal for you. Even if you've only been able to carve out some time to work on your book on a regular basis, I am proud of you. The most important thing is the journey has begun.

One of the main concepts of the *Writing a Book God's Way* book writing program includes excavating your unique groups of existing knowledge and opinions. Many people think they have to be super smart while doing tons of research on a topic they barely know anything about much less feel any passion for.

There are two schools of thought on this; one says you need to be passionate about your topic and write only about what you know. The other thinkers say you must find a topic that fills a desperate need.

I espouse both sides; but I prefer the passion based book. I've written books that fill a need and I write books that light my fire and lights the fire of my readers. A student of mine said, "Why not choose a topic you're passionate about and seek to fill a great need in that area?" There you have it; I agree.

Anyway, following this program you will pull out modules or nuggets from existing information from your speeches, sermons, Bible classes, courses, articles, brochures. If you've never done this before, you may be surprised at what turns up.

When you organize your information into groups and categories, it will be easier to write your book and easier to repackage your ideas into newsletters, articles, speeches and website reports that will help market and sell your book.

These nugget ideas in its various forms will engage your readers and build your credibility. With anything valuable such as gold, the sifting process will reveal the rough cut form (draft). Then a process called refining is used where heat is applied to purify and even re-shape and polish the gold to its fullest potential.

So it is with your collection of knowledge and experiences. Sift through your files and memories looking for nuggets (groups of pertinent information) you can identify, organize and write about. Then apply the heat of purging unnecessary information.

Burn away all the dross and impurities of your message by tossing the unrelated information. By grouping and categorizing your existing knowledge, you can identify and list chapter titles and even main supporting points. The result will be a fast and easy writing of your book.

So I encourage you to keep going in this course; I have more to say to you about getting started and sticking with it until you finish. Onward march...let's start mining your background and experiences for book gold!

MINE YOUR KNOWLEDGE AND EXPERIENCES LIKE GOLD

Writing can be a joy-filled creative process to some and a drudgery-filled chore to others. According to Roger C. Parker, "Writing is more a process of identification and organization than the relatively mechanical process of selecting words and placing them in sentences and paragraphs."

My goal is to help you to see writing your book quickly is

simply a matter of harvesting your information and recognizing that you probably already possess the majority of the information needed to complete your book.

The real test is simply to organize what you know into a database of usable ideas. The steps outlined in this chapter will help you identify and organize the information you need (and already have) into chunks of information to write your book. By analyzing your experiences and life observations into building block ideas and using a table to organize them, you will be ready to write sooner.

By implementing the following steps of identifying and organizing your ideas, you will easily write and complete your book. To start do this:

1. **Realize you know more than you think.**

You have gained a certain level of success in your field, career or even hobby. You may be an active consultant, business owner, speaker, or writer. In your field you have been constantly learning and observing. On your path to success through failures, successes and opportunities to learn, you have been accumulating the information you need to complete your book.

You have experienced and observed what works and does not work. You have developed over time an understanding of what order things should happen and how it appears out of order when it doesn't happen in that order. Through the process of continually doing what you do, you have gained a wealth of knowledge and information.

The challenge is that your knowledge is unorganized. Once you create a structure for organizing your ideas, your ability to create your book and/or books will quickly take shape.

2. **Divide and conquer**

Mark Twain said it best, "Nothing is particularly hard if you divide it into small jobs." Begin to break your knowledge into chunks of information. The beginning point is to begin separate your files, speeches, articles into general topics. For example, I have bodies of information for my inspirational writing and a whole other body or topic for business writing.

And of course there's another topic for the how-tos of writing in my files. When I first started, I went through and separated these chunks of information into different folders and eventually as my chunks of information grew I had to house them in separate file units.

After creating topical groups, break your knowledge for your book into individual ideas or chunks of information so you can inventory what you already know on the subject.

You'll notice as you organize and inventory the ideas you already possess; it will uncover some areas that your knowledge is a bit weak. Once you identify the weak areas in your knowledge, it becomes easy to locate the information needed to fill in the gap or strengthen the weak area.

3. **Create framework for organizing your ideas**

For a short book, simply create a list of every idea related to your book's topic. Once you start your list and create a structure you'll be surprised at how quickly your book takes shape. Now take your list and number them in order of importance. After your ideas have been prioritized, you can easily spot patterns of what will lead to writing a book on what you are most passionate about.

4. **Pursue your most passionate idea**

For now, put aside your list of topics. Take a break and relax. Successful books are based on one central idea. The author concentrates on one main theme to drive their book to success. Textbooks can get away with a list of all kinds of facts. But non-fiction books, especially how-to books are based on one main idea.

The central idea provides the focus needed to make your writing compelling. For your book, you need a viewpoint, a position, and a conclusion that you develop fact by fact or step by step as you write. .Readers look for an easy read. They look for a book that will help them solve their problem step by step. They need interpretation, perspective and sequence.

The easiest way to come up with a main idea for your book is to follow your passion. To choose a subject that you will be still be passionate about in a year or so, ask yourself these questions:

What ideas am I really passionate about? What ideas do I consistently discuss no matter where I am? What ideas do I really want to share with the world? Where do I see others making the same mistakes I did? How can I help people with my knowledge? What key ideas helped me succeed or caused me to fail? What main idea can make a difference in the lives of others?

The main idea for your book may come to you when you least expect it. So over the next few days begin to mull it over in your mind. Spend some quiet time, if only for a few minutes during the day to think about your deep passion, your mission, the idea that really moves you. This is important because if you pinpoint your passion well, the easier it will be to write a book that expresses what you want to express.

Readers enjoy and appreciate passion. When you are excited about a topic, your enthusiasm and excitement is contagious. Your readers will connect to you and be excited by it. They will reward you by reading your book from cover to cover and then tell all their friends about your wonderful, insightful book.

It's important to note the more passionate you are about your topic the faster you will be able to write, complete and publish your book.

5. Excavate Your Background

As you look for ideas, don't leave out reviewing your work history and/or volunteer history and create another list. Note any boards you have served on. Examine the associations and organizations you have been a member of over the years.

Organize this one by employer, client, and organization.

Examine every job, client and task. Think about things you learned. What mistakes did you observe? What procedures did you learn? What were the pros and cons of the relationship? Examine all successes and failures. What were any lessons learned? Make a note of what you feel you gained from each experience with a job, client or organization.

6. **Re-examine the files full of your writing and speaking**

Even if you are not published yet, you probably have a lot more knowledge stored that you have written or created than you realize. As a professional, you have written memos, proposals and reports. You may have conducted meetings, delivered presentations and speeches or short talks. These may all contain valuable information which you have forgotten.

Make another list and write down the title or topic of every article, proposal, report or presentation that you have ever given. Next to the topic or title write down the main idea that you developed in them.

Then skim the actual report, speech or article and look for relevant nuggets of information that you can re-use. Dissect each piece for ideas that should be added to your topic.

7. **Create a System**

The process of checking your background for ideas should be continuous. As you write your book, you will find yourself continuing the process of organizing and re-organizing your ideas. Take your list of ideas and add any nuggets you located while reviewing your background, speeches and articles.

As you progress, new ideas will come to you. It's o.k. to jot your ideas down on a piece of paper until you have a chance to file it. But for some of us, our desk can quickly become a hodge-podge of sticky notes and scraps of paper. Now is the time to create your system that you will use throughout writing your book. Judy Cullins puts it like this, "Stop Piling and Start Filing."

Research experts say over 150 hours a year is wasted looking for misplaced paper. Organization is key because the Pareto Time Management says that only 10% of our papers are actually important.

I suggest creating a hard copy file and computer file version for your book. I realize some may favor the hard copy and some may favor the computer system. Ultimately, I don't think it matters that much which one you choose as long as you setup a system that works for you.

For the hard copy version of your book files, make one vertical or hanging folder for your book. Then take one manila folder for each chapter and label it with chapter's shortened name. Take one manila folder for each part of your book: front matter, back matter and even promotion or marketing folder. When you give each part of your book a place in your book file, you will find it fast and write your book fast.

8. **Fill In the Weak Spots of Your Existing Knowledge**

As you begin to uncover your nuggets and chunks of knowledge related to your central idea or concept you will uncover areas where you are missing supporting information. Now is the time to locate it. The starting point for research is your local library, bookstore and the Internet. Guard against plagiarizing the work of others, but identify areas you need to explore further to gain facts and ideas that support your book's theme.

Avid readers make the best writers. If not already, develop or strengthen your habit of reading. For your book writing project, begin to analyze what you read. Look for books that relate to your topic and read them. Take note of the ones you like the best. Analyze what made them easy to read or what set them apart from the others. Also, take note of any new ideas you come across.

Mining the gold called **your knowledge** starts by recognizing that you probably already possess most of the information you need to complete your unique book. Using the principles of organizing and prioritizing it outlined in this chapter, you will quickly have the bare bones of your book in hand. By analyzing your background and observations to the core ideas and organizing them, you will write and complete your book faster than ever dreamed.

DIG A LITTLE DEEPER AND PUT YOUR EXPERT KNOWLEDGE TO WORK FOR YOU

Again, I believe you already have what it takes to write your book. And like other successful Christian authors you can create or increase your passive income stream each month. Your professional competitors wish you would never discover these secrets.

You may be asking "What if I'm not a professional writer?" You can still write your professional book and start earning in a few months. I am convinced your audience is waiting on your insightful expertise to help solve their problems.

All it takes is a little know how to write your book like a pro. Start by solving your readers' problems using your expert knowledge. You know the counselling sessions and the Bible classes you already taught. Use the articles, speeches and reports already in your files.

Expand one of your articles or speeches into a short book by adding short stories and some practical how-to steps. If you want to write your book like a pro and increase your income, read these five secrets and apply them:

1. Secret One. Write a short book first to build your confidence.

I know short doesn't mean the same thing to every person. For books, let's agree 50-100 or so pages is short, even 140 sounds less intimidating than a 200-300 page book. Your future customers are busy and usually read only what takes the shortest amount of time. For example, a friend of mine wanted to learn how to conduct tele-seminars. He said he didn't hesitate buying a short book at $19.97 to teach him the ropes of tele-seminars.

Make your book simpler, shorter, and punchier. Shorten your sentences, stories and analogies. Your professional format will include a strong heading (question) your reader needs answered and the answer. This professional formula presents the problem and solution quickly without a lot of words.

2. Secret Two. Focus on one topic in your book.

It's a known fact bestsellers focus on one main topic. Focus on one topic then write each chapter to support that subject. When you overload your reader with information, you come across as disorganized, wordy and flat. Instead of including everything you know, stick to one how-to subject and include plenty of simple details with examples to make it useful to your reader.

3. Secret Three. Brand yourself, your business and your book. Think about the greatest benefit that you offer through your book or service. Consider your book and chapter titles. Now think about your keywords and headings on your website. Do you see a repeating word that stands out?

For example, the book "Win With the Writer Inside You" the author threads some form of "win" throughout her materials. Ever heard of the Chicken Soup for the Soul series? The title changes in its audience but the Chicken Soup brand stays the same. For example, there's a Chicken Soup for Teen-agers, Chicken Soup for Mothers, and so on.

4. Secret Four. Get a professional editor or book coach.

Yes, its o.k. and you should get feedback from family, friends, local writing group, etc. But you need to get a professional viewpoint of your work to weed out the passive voice, bad grammar and all the things that slow your readers down to a standstill.

Copy that appeals to the emotions of your reader sell your books. Your future customers want word pictures that they can respond to with their emotions.

5. Secret Five. Target and get to know your audience.

Let's face it not everyone will want to read your book. Most uninformed authors write what they feel is a great book; spend tons of time and sometimes money looking for people to buy it. Instead match your expert knowledge with an audience you can serve.

Consider their needs, problems and how you can help solve them. Business people are a hot audience right now. They are hungry and willing to buy what will improve, make profitable their life and business. Right now think of one to three preferred audiences in your area of expertise. Then write the book your customers will be looking for.

It's faster to write a book if you know how. People are looking for practical information and knowledge that you have. Don't let your ideas, knowledge and expertise fade away. Put it to work for you in a book. Remember, if you need help contact a professional book coach or take an e-course to inform yourself.

THIS WEEK'S ASSIGNMENT

1) Gather all the information you have about your chosen topic and begin to sift. Divide what you come up with into chunks. Even if you've begun writing, do this. It will lead to faster book writing for the rest of your book and future books. Create a list of topics and sections for your book. Possible ideas for book 2 or other books may even emerge…If so, label and file this information into a separate folder.

____

____

____

2) Get organized. Designate 1 large folder or file cabinet to your book project(s). Make file folders for each of your chapters. File everything that has to do with your book into these folders.

Yes, every little piece of paper related to your book must be filed. Remember, you are preparing to write fast. No more wasting 150 hours per year looking for misplaced information, right.

____

____

____

WORDS WORTH REMEMBERING:

We are not in the position in which we have nothing to work with. We already have capacities, talents, missions, callings.

—Abraham Moslow

Coming Up Next ...

Chapter 9: *How to Build a Saleable Book*

In the next lesson, we'll discuss how to create a chapter template & start putting content into your book. Don't worry its easy; it's kind of like building your favorite taco. Also, copy the chapter template I've included as a gift to help you structure your chapters.

CHAPTER 9

How To Build A Saleable Book

For which of you, wishing to build a farm-building, does not first sit down and calculate the cost, whether he has sufficient means to finish it?
—Luke 14:28

The best non-fiction books have a set structure to house their chapters. That structure provides the framework for each chapter. It's stressful to re-invent the wheel every time with a blank screen.

Most people including the author are intimidated by a blank screen. Instead of starting from scratch each chapter, use repeating elements to create structure. In *John Maxwell's* "21 Irrefutable Laws of Leadership: Follow Them and People Will Follow You" foreword by *Zig Ziglar* contains repeating elements that house each chapter.

Each chapter has the same basic form. I know I alluded in the last lesson preview that it was kind of like building a taco. You start with your favorite corn or flour taco shell; then you add meat, lettuce, tomato, cilantro, taco sauce and sour cream…And yes this is true.

But after communicating with some of you as students, I'll stick with my first analogy of building a house. We laid the foundation, now we're ready to do the framework. After the framework, you start step by step adding to your house. In a similar way, after we've developed the chapter template, we will fill our book with content and all the book parts you've already developed to slide in place. So, without further ado let's get started on building your book...

HOW TO BUILD A BOOK FAST!

Have you been trying to re-invent the wheel with each attempt to write your book? It can be stressful staring at a blank screen. Putting this chapter into action will set the stage for the rest of your book. You might be surprised at how easy and stress-free completing your book becomes.

Readers enjoy easy-to-read maps to guide them through your book. They love consistency. It is disconcerting and unprofessional if you change formats throughout the book. In non-fiction books, each chapter should be similar length and have same sections or categories. Then to make your chapters come alive, use engagement tools such as anecdotes, human interest stories, case studies, sizzling headings, pull quotes, bulleted lists, photos, maps, graphs, exercises, short tips. Also, readers enjoy easy-to-read side bars and/or small sections in boxes.

But first you must create an outline to structure your chapters and then fill in the blanks as you work on your book. The best non-fiction books have a set structure to house each chapter. Use repeating elements in each chapter. Your readers will love knowing generally what to expect in each chapter and reward you by reading your book from start to finish.

Do as John Maxwell and other successful authors did and use repeating elements to create structure. In John Maxwell's "21 Irrefutable Laws of Leadership" each chapter contained the same basic form. The author included a chapter title, brief quote, and list of supporting points, introduction, basic lesson principle and conclusion. For starters, each of your chapters should contain at least eight of the eleven points below:

1. *Chapter Title:* The title immediately followed by a subtitle emphasizes and explains its meaning.

2. *Brief Quote:* Follow each title with one or two quotes related to the topic of your book. You may pull the quote from your speeches, classes, studies or other authorities in your field which support the title. Everyone enjoys a short impactful statement that will add interest to your book. Additionally, it's an automatic increase to your credibility. It shows you did some research for your book.

3. *Introduction:* Each chapter begins with 5-8 paragraphs of introduction that may include a story presenting the chapter's main principle or underlying theme. For short books 1 to 4 paragraphs sounds great.

4. *Seven to Ten Points.* Follow the introduction with lessons or tools to achieve the goal presented in the introduction. Condense your material as you develop each point. Some lessons will require one paragraph and others may need several.

5. *Pull-Outs or Pull Quotes:* Put in short warnings, tips or resources that are relevant to the chapter. Often, pull quotes are inserted in a shaded box or larger font type with quotations around it.

6. *Sidebars.* Sidebars are similar to pull-quotes in that they take you aside from the normal flow of text. They are short, three to five paragraph in-depth discussion of a particular topic that is lightly discussed in the main body of each chapter.

   Besides adding visual interest, they allow the

author to discuss a topic in detail that if included in the regular text flow, would slow down the reader with too much information.

7. *Case Studies.* Include one or more stories in each chapter. Or form a case study or exhibit that supports the chapter's theme.
8. *Self-Evaluation Tools.* Include brief questions that permit your readers to measure their progress with each of the principles described in each chapter.
9. *Conclusion.* Close each chapter with four to eight paragraphs that summarize the central ideas and supporting points. The conclusion can also lead the way or contain a transitional element to a future chapter by previewing the topic discussed in the next chapter.
10. *Glossary.* Glossaries are lists containing definitions of terms introduced for the first time in each chapter. Glossaries help beginners better understand the adjacent text.
11. *Notes and/or Bibliography.* These lists are usually inserted at the end of the book providing reference notes or bibliography credits to authors and books the author used for research.

You may include or not include all of the elements above. Most importantly, is to be consistent. For a solid structure to start your house, remember to include your chapter title, brief quote or statement, introduction, seven to ten tips or lessons, case study, engagement tools and a conclusion.

Your readers will enjoy your well structured book and reward you by reading it from start to finish. Then they will tell all their friends and recommend they read your easy-to-read, insightful, useful book.

DEVELOP ENGAGEMENT TOOLS

Add value and interest to your chapters by including other engagement tools. Sprinkle interesting ways for your reader to interact with your material. For example, include worksheets, note sheets and lists to engage your readers and make them an active participant.

Your engagement tool can be as simple as a set of review questions at the end of each chapter to encourage thoughtful reflections of the points covered in the chapter. Checklist and worksheets are the two most common engagement tools. Checklists provide a framework for readers to answer questions, define their goals and identify available resources. Worksheets also help readers measure their progress with applying the principles in your book.

CREATE A CHAPTER TEMPLATE

After you have outlined or structured your book with the repeating elements in each chapter, create a template which will form the basis of each chapter.

For longer books, you should create a separate template file named after each chapter. i.e. "03 chapter passion points." For shorter books, I just create separate pages for each chapter.

After creating the template file or page, go through and insert placeholder text for each element of the chapter. For example, the chapter template for one of my books looked like this:

Chapter Number

Chapter Title

Quote

Lesson Outline or Key Points

Introduction

Principle 1

Principle 2

Principle 3

Principle 4

Principle 5

Conclusion

Review Questions

REVIEW CHAPTER POINTS

After creating this chapter template and using my table of contents, I could easily go through and insert key points. In the organization stage, I may go through and insert the key points of each chapter into the template.

When I began working on the writing stage, I would easily go to the chapter template write supporting paragraphs using the key points already inserted.

Chapter titles and subtitles are similar to book titles and subtitles. You will use the same title writing skills gained in *Lesson Seven "Book Titles Sell Books"* to craft your chapter titles and subtitles.

Review your chapter titles and outline (table of contents) you identified in the planning stage. As you review, make sure each chapter contributes to the overall theme of your book. Does it support your book's goal or the benefit, or promise made in the book's title.

Each chapter should reflect one step towards the title promise. For example, each lesson represents a single step in the 12 week book writing program promised in this course's title and subtitle. Write Your Best Book Now: Book Writing Course – How to Write a Book In 100 Days or Less.

If after reviewing, you discover the chapters do not support your title. Don't stress, just revise, and reorganize until it does. Changes in this stage are common. You may discover you left out a topic or end up with an awkward number of topics. With a little work and revision you will end up with a more sound structure and flow.

FILE MANAGEMENT

For longer books, create a separate folder for your book and each chapter. Create a hard copy file folder and a computer folder in your directory list. In Microsoft Word select 'Save As' under File. Go to *My Documents* and create a folder name after your book or use the initials. For example BWC might be a good folder name for the course. Put all your book related files in this folder.

For shorter version books, make sure you create a separate folder for your book; you can easily find it when you are ready to work. If you create a template that includes placeholder text for the elements to be included in each chapter of your book, you will simplify your book writing process. By creating files and inserting first draft key points and topics identified while creating your book marketing plan, you will gain a major jumpstart.

Then each time you open a chapter template, you can easily see where you are and what needs work. By printing out each chapter – even if it's just placeholder text right now, you can easily jot down ideas that you want to include in the chapter.

LIST OF ENGAGEMENTS TOOLS

You can include one of these in your chapter or mix and match. Try not to overdo it.

1. *Checklist.* Create a list of things to check for a particular process related to your book's topic. Ex.: a checklist of

things to consider when choosing a POD publisher.

2. *Templates.* Design a template that will make a certain action easier for your readers. Ex.: a template for writing a newsletter.
3. *Dictionary of Terms.* Publish a web directory or ebook dictionary of terms related to your specific book's topic.
4. *Study-Guide* (mini) Format the information in a summarized style and add questions for each book chapter or section.
5. *Questions & Answers Session.* Get permission to publish a question and answer session you've done to illustrate a point in the book.
6. *Worksheets.* Create a mini worksheet with fill in the blank format. Your reader can read the chapter then fill out the worksheet at the end of chapter.
7. *Space to write or journal.* Leave a well designed space or blank lines at the end of each chapter for your reader to write down their thoughts or journal.
8. *Pull Quotes.* Create a small box with an interesting quote from the book content or an inspirational quote related to content.
9. *Sidebar.* Create a larger box for material needed to explain but will slow down your reader if left in regular flow of text.
10. *Tips Box.* A box similar to the pull quote but this box contains a short interesting tip.
11. *Dictionary of related terms.* Create a glossary or list of terms used in book that need further explanation.
12. *Ready made plans.* Create ready-made plans for a

particular project your book's targeted audience wants to accomplish. It could be a diet plan, marketing plan, landscape plan, etc.

13. *Directory of resources.* Develop a list of resources that your audience could use to go get extra stuff related to your book content.
14. *Case studies.* Use short stories about your customer's experience with you or the successful results of them using your information.
15. *Invitation to download something at companion website.* Direct your reader to your book's companion website to download a free gift or sign-up for extra resources from you. You may recognize this one from this book. All throughout the book, I've been inviting you to visit our companion website at http://www.bookwritingcourse.com.

Chapter Template (Visit http://www.bookwritingcourse.com/specialoffer.htm to download full version book template and other bonus reports available to *Writing a Book God's Way In 100 Days* book owners.)

Chapter One

Chapter Title
Nice quotation
Introduction

1. Chapter supporting points, tips, lessons
2. Chapter supporting points
3. Chapter supporting points
4. Chapter supporting points
5. Chapter supporting points
6. Chapter supporting points
7. Chapter supporting points

Chapter summary

THIS WEEK'S ASSIGNMENT

1) Create your chapter template. Develop your chapter format. If you have 7 chapters, setup a template for each chapter within one Word doc file. For example, each chapter will have a place holder for chapter title, quote (interesting fact), introduction, main point or solution, supporting facts, summary or provocative questions and end of chapter. You can use the chapter template that came with this lesson.

---

2) Choose 2 or more engagement tools to use in your book. List them below. Explain how you plan to use them.

---

3) Take the blocks and sections of information you pulled from your speeches, articles, notes, research, any body of information related and put it into your chapter template. At this point, it doesn't matter if it's in the final order. Match each body of information with your TOC that you completed in an earlier lesson.

WORDS WORTH REMEMBERING:

Nothing is particularly hard if you divide it into small jobs.

—Mark Twain

Coming Up Next ...

Chapter 10: *Finishing Your Book Faster and Selling Sooner*
In the next lesson, we'll explore how to write a book faster and go to market sooner. I'll give you some insider techniques that are sure to speed up your writing.

CHAPTER 10

Finishing A Book Faster And Selling Sooner

He who observes the wind (and waits for all conditions to be favorable) will not sow, and he who regards the clouds will not reap.
—Ecclesiastes 11:4

You can write a book faster if you know how. I don't say that facetiously; because I'm about to teach you how to write your book faster in less time. I believe people are looking for practical information and knowledge that you have. Don't let your ideas, knowledge and expertise fade away.

Keep going in this course; put your ideas to work for you in a book. Remember; if you need extra help consider the personalized one-on-one coaching located below. http://www.bookwritingcourse.com/roundtable.htm

Have you been guilty of procrastinating on your book project, lately? If you're anything like I was, you may have gotten hung up with wrong thinking about writing and completing your book.

In the lesson below, knowledge and know-how is formed into ten myth busters that will destroy the power of procrastination, forever. Anyone, can use the amazingly easy steps below to conquer the giant procrastination and speedily write their book.

Even so, nothing can happen until that first draft is completed. Remember procrastination is ultimately based on fear of failure. It has stopped countless of book projects and stolen the vision of many more. Don't allow procrastination to become a giant towering over your book dreams. Let's keep going together to the finish line...

Many speakers, consultants, professionals and small business owners alike feel confident with communicating their message orally. They can spout their message in an elevator speech with the accuracy of a scientist. But when it comes to putting it on paper, some grown men & women end up crying like a baby.

Through speaking and writing, I have discovered 10 myths that often block and slow the progress of others from completing their book fast. I promise. It's not hard once you know exactly what to do. Successful writers set up a system of writing. Destroy these myths and setup your system of writing and write your book fast.

Myth 1: My book is not a product; it's personal even a work of art.

Do a reality check! Treat your book as a business. It was one thing to write your family's history book. You had no plans of marketing it to the world. It's another thing to write a book about a topic in your field. Your expectations are different and quite higher. If marketed correctly, you can expect your book about a topic in your field to brand your business; it can make you a sought after expert and draw hundreds of new clients.

Set your book up to succeed with a book marketing plan. Your book marketing plan is what I describe as your map. It describes your book, what you will do after the book is completed and published. It also describes who you hope to sell your book to a target audience. In short you can say your book marketing plan is your roadmap to success and profits.

Myth 2: Later is better than now.

Create a sense of urgency! Many less determined writers get discouraged and quit because their book journey is not as easy and fast as they thought. May I gently say, "Get over it!" Most worthwhile endeavors take perseverance and hard work. Here's a different perspective; the attention, direction and intent it takes to overcome most obstacles can be developed into new strengths and skills.

Act now. Too many of us for too long have hid behind the words, "It's too hard." Now is the time to take charge of our fears and conquer them. First things first, to overcome procrastination -the fear of failure- is to act now. Most times the bottom line of procrastination is fear of failure.

If your schedule hasn't permitted you to follow this course exactly, don't give up. You can go back anytime and follow the exercises to a saleable book. Remember, action will destroy fear. Each successful step of your system will deal a death blow to fear.

Myth 3: I need to become a hermit for a year.

Avoid marathon writing. Have you thought, "I have to get away from everything to write a successful book?" No you don't. I know several novelist and non-fiction book writers who had to write during a long commute to get their best book written and out to the world.

They accomplished it because they systematically worked on their book until it was done. In the midst of your busy life, designate your time to write (work on your book) with a goal to completion. (reasonable time to completion)

Myth 4: I can't keep up with where I am after interruptions of life.

Keep going after life interrupts. Set yourself up for success; use the tracking approach. I can't keep up with where I am after interruptions of life. It is a common challenge to find your place after being interrupted with family, work and daily life. After all that's why many think you must get away to get it done effectively.

Yet, there's hope for those who can't get away or choose not to. Successful writers all over the world use the tracking approach. They succeed because they commit to doing a little each day.

There are 2 methods you could use for your tracking. Time is the method where you commit to a writing a certain amount of time each day. With the cumulative factor involved your commitment doesn't have to be that much.

For example, to accomplish my book writing goals I commit to writing one hour a day in my most productive time. For me it is right after my meditation and reading time. With this method don't be overly concerned about how much you write, just keep the time commitment.

The other method is focused on output. Commit to writing a certain number of words or pages a day, perhaps 750-1,000 words or approximately three and a half pages double-spaced text. The key factor is to stick to it until completion.

Winner's Note: You may ask how do I get started after interruptions or even in my daily allotted slot so that I don't spend a lot of time re-locating where I stopped? Start your daily writing session by re-reading the last words you wrote the day before. This will get you back in the flow. The continued cycle of review will create a momentum that will keep you going to completion. Another piece of advice, is to create a support system that will help isolate you from telephone calls and interruptions during your daily Tracking Session.

Myth 5: I must write my book in order.

Find your writing rhythm. Don't become chained to writing in order. Jump around and fill in the blanks. Review your chapters and whatever subject or topic you most drawn to, begin there. Many inexperienced writers feel they have to complete each chapter in order.

It's called linear writing (writing each chapter in order.) You don't have to write each chapter one after the other. If you happen to get stuck on chapter two, you could be stuck a very long time. I think this type of thinking comes from grade school where we are ritually taught to do everything in order.

If you have been thinking that way stop right now, no need to raise your hand. You have my permission to work on whatever chapter moves you or you feel passion bubbling for at the moment. Feeling stuck on a chapter, try another. There you have it now go with the flow.

Myth 6: When I get writers block, I have to stop writing until I feel it again.

Maintain your momentum; keep your writing commitments. Do your ever feel like I am stuck. I have to stop writing until I feel it again. Don't worry many of us have felt that way. From what I said earlier you may have gotten the impression that you just write when you feel like it and quit when you don't. If so, no that's not what I meant.

Unseasoned writers may play the martyr and push through just to put something on paper or give up and try again another day. We would never get it done like that. When you get stuck simply close that chapter and pull out your chapter outline and choose another chapter.

If you have been following this book writing course, you may have listed main points for each lesson. Select a topic from that chapter and begin there. Go around writer's block by working on another chapter.

For example, while writing this course in one of my writing sessions, I wanted to finish seventh lesson on titles but I ran into a writer's block. Instead of breaking my momentum, I came down to lesson ten about easy writing and began there. I was able to complete my time commitment of one hour and keep my momentum.

Myth 7: I never have to rewrite or I think I have to rewrite constantly.

Many newbie and seasoned writers alike are perfectionist. So, you'll find both writers who pendulum between the above mindsets of never rewriting or rewriting constantly. My best advice is to turn off the editor mindset when writing. When writing, many feel the urge to stop and change something every few paragraphs. Or they finish a page and want to perfect it before continuing. Turn off your editor voice while writing your first draft. Your goal should be to get the message on paper.

Avoid re-writing during your first draft. After your message is written completely out, then you can turn the editor's voice back up. It's true successful authors rewrite and organize their ideas for the strongest impact. But in the beginning stages of writing your book, concentrate on finishing each chapter. Use later writing sessions to self-edit. When it's time to edit, check your ideas for flow, grammar, spelling, and chapter endings. Work on your chapter titles and lead in introductions.

Myth 8: I have to do it ALL myself.

Learn to delegate and share faster and faster. Don't succumb to the feeling that you have to do it all yourself. As writers, we can get pretty isolated in our thinking if we're not careful. Do your research and reading time apart from your writing sessions. You may be able to ask your spouse, a teen-aged son or daughter, a friend to help with your research.

Know when to let go of your chapters and book. Don't self-edit and pick your book apart word by word. Learn to use your skills at the highest level possible. Some of the mechanical tasks of proofreading ask a family member, part-time employee or again a friend to help.

After you have done the best job you can with your manuscript, don't be afraid to pass it to a professional. Learn to delegate faster and faster.

Myth 9: I don't know how to use a computer so I can't write my book.

Value your time. Learn how to do it easier and faster. Many of my clients and students have said, "I don't know anything about computers so pecking my book out would probably take forever." My response is always the same. Don't run from technology.

At least take the time to learn about the shortcuts in your current software. Welcome to the new millennium! Embrace technology; make your software work efficiently for you. If you truly are hindered by not knowing your current software, take a class to begin using your software. No time for a class, hire an assistant or outsource the portion where your skill is weak.

Myth 10: I'll never lose my work; so I don't need to form a habit of backing up.

Develop the habit now to save your work and print daily. Many of us think computer crashes, loss of information would never happen to us until it does. If you have been computing long, you know computer crashes or loss of data can happen to anyone. Don't take the chance of losing your hard work. Print out and back up daily.

Save your manuscript to an alternate space. Use a travel disc drive (jump drive) or burn a cd of your book files. Safeguard your time investment; backup today and every day.

Writing a book is a journey. Most journeys go so much smoother with a system in place. Taking the simple steps above will get you started fast and keep you going to completion. Start today then complete and release your significant message to the world.

21 WEEKEND WARRIOR BOOK WRITING TIPS
How to Write a Book Using Small Blocks of Time

Are you only able to work on your book project on the weekend or in small blocks of time? No worries. Welcome to the *Weekend Warrior Book Writing Club*! No, you don't have to pay dues to join. You need only be a person struggling to fit book writing into a small block of time.

You may be weary with the start and stops most busy professionals, home business owners or care takers have to deal with. Take it from a fellow weekend warrior book writer, you can do it! You do the hard stuff all day long. I'm convinced you can get focused, fit it in and finish your book this year. Your audience is waiting to read your insightful book.

But first the pep talk, think about all the benefits you are missing by not fulfilling your book dream. Let's put a time table to that thought. What would happen if you didn't get your short book written in the next 100 days? You'd miss having a book to make your business stand out in the crowd. Your business would definitely take longer to build to a whopper success.

You wouldn't have the competitive edge you'd have as an expert with a book. You'd miss out on the adventures and opportunities waiting for you on the other side of getting your book done. And worst of all, you'd miss the extra profits you could make by charging up to 400% more on your fees as author.

Now that you are properly motivated to cash in on all that you are missing by not getting your book done. Here are 21 simple strategies to get your book written using your weekends or any small blocks of time.

1. **Take a load off your mind.**

   Remove the pressure to complete a big book. Instead choose to write a short book. Divide your monster size book into 2 books. Use shorter sentences and paragraphs. Your copy is more compelling when you are succinct and to the point. Write shorter chapters; shorten your stories and examples. Make your book an easy read. If you have a fairly complex topic, spread out your stats and tables. Section your details and develop your book into several parts.

2. **Focus on one topic in your book.**

   It's easier to focus on one topic. In book writing and most things easier translates to faster. Plus, it's a known fact bestsellers focus on one main topic. Focus on one topic then write each chapter to support that subject. When you overload your reader with information, you come across as disorganized, wordy and flat. Instead of including everything you know, stick to one how-to subject and include plenty of simple details with examples and stories to make it useful to your reader.

3. **Put your book as a top priority.**

   Commit to a writing schedule. Think about your priorities right now. Through this course, have you arranged to write at least 15-20 hours a week? If you have to let something go that is not high on your priority list, do it. Now is your time to succeed in writing your book. Later is not better. Set yourself up for success. Write a book this year by making your book goal a top priority.

4. **Target and get to know your audience.**

   Let's face it not everyone will want to read your book. Most uninformed authors write what they feel is a great book; spend tons of time and sometimes money looking for people to buy it. Instead match your expert knowledge with an audience you can serve.

   Consider their needs, problems and how you can help solve them. Business people are a hot audience right now. They are hungry and willing to buy what will improve, make profitable their life and business. Right now think of one to three preferred audiences in your area of expertise. Make it easy on yourself; choose one. Then write the book your customers will be looking for.

5. **Write with an intention statement.**

   Do you have a plan in place? Write on purpose. Don't set yourself up to fail by not planning. Even if it's a simple intention goal like "I complete my book (title of book) this year by (date and year.) I educate myself and do what it takes to complete it." Set one and write it down so you can hit the mark.

6. **Write the easy way to finish fast.**

   In the previous lesson, I mentioned the five top ways to speed write your book includes: 1.*Act Now.* Action will paralyze fear each and every time. 2. *Avoid marathon writing.* Know you don't have to become a hermit to write and complete a successful book. 3. *Commit to the tracking approach.*

   Doing a set amount –even if it's only 30 minutes to an hour- each day builds a cumulative effect. 4. *Know you don't have to write chapters in order.* You can jump around and fill in the blanks to gain momentum. 5. *Maintain your momentum.*

Don't give in to writers block. Move on to work on the chapter you feel passion bubbling for at that moment.

7. **Write using laser focus.**

Apply laser focus to complete your book writing project faster. For example, if you look at a 40 watt bulb, the light is soft. It's not even strong enough to light an average room sufficiently. Yet you can take the same 40 watts; put it in a laser gun and get a totally different output.

In the laser gun, the same 40 watts become a focused beam of light that can cut through different objects like a sharp knife through paper. Same amount of energy but different focus. To use laser focus in your book project, prioritize, do only one project at a time and complete one project before you start another.

8. **Break writing into short sections.**

It's easier on you to write in short blocks of time. Furthermore, it's easier on your reader to read. Try to break long paragraphs into shorter, more digestible chunks. Later you can work on making these chunks flow as one unit or chapter. Make it easy to read and you'll reach more readers.

9. **Write short sentences and use simple words.**

Writing and reading a long sentence takes longer than a short one. Cut lengthy sentences in half to make your writing easier to read. Aim your copy so a 7th -8th grader could understand it. Remember using complex words won't impress your readers. Most times it will annoy them to the point of not finishing your book.

10. **Cut wordiness but be specific.**

Compelling books are concise. Unnecessary words waste your time and most of all your reader's time. It dilutes your message and makes your book longer than necessary. Additionally, be specific. When writing your book, stick to the specific information about your topic. The more relevant facts you include, the better. If you don't bother to dig for specifics about your topic, your book may end up vague filled with meaningless words that few people read.

11. **Create a book in an electronic format.**

First, ebooks are not dead. There are still many selling lots of ebooks each year, including the author. Put your message in a downloadable file to sell. Top selling ebooks are normally shorter and more specialized. You can publish your book as an ebook first or compile an ebook version of your existing print book. Don't delay any longer, write your short book and put it in a (PDF) to sell to your website visitors.

12. **Use your existing body of knowledge.**

Even if you add more researched information later, start with your existing knowledge first. Pull from your speeches, workshops, work experiences, etc. You may have collected a body of information just for fun. Or you did a bunch of research to make a business decision. For example, when I published my first book I gathered detailed information about POD publishing service companies and vendors to make the best decision.

I later compiled that information into a free report and gave it away to hundreds promoting my website. Over the years, I added to that body of information and it grew into a self publishing resource website. Then finally, I added enough that I developed it into a book about self publishing.

13. **Write in an organized way.**

Leading experts say we waste over 150 hours a year looking for misplaced information. Get organized in a way that fits you. For example, to get started you can create a master folder with your book's title. Inside, keep a separate file for each chapter. Assign each chapter a short title that will make sense later. If you don't have a title yet then assign chapter names by topic.

Assign research notes or resources to each chapter named folder. Make a how-to folder as well, such as short-key notes, style or formatting notes. With this system you can manage multiple projects easily. Don't waste anymore time being disorganized. Remember you only have weekends and small blocks of time to complete. You can do it; just get organized.

14. **Write a clear thesis.**

Did you cringe at the word thesis? For some, it brought back memories of English class and writing essays. No worries, a thesis simply reflects the main central thought of the book. Make sure the main central thought includes the greatest benefit of your book and you're done.

Writing your book's thesis before you begin will help crystallize your message. With your book's thesis in mind, you can stay on the path of focused, compelling yet easy to read book. You could end up with a top selling book written on the weekends all because your message was tightly focused.

15. **Write with extreme focus.**

Throw away your plans to go away for a week, a month or a year to write your book. Weekend warriors don't have the time to dedicate solely to their book. So, i*t's a good thing* you don't have to become a hermit to write and complete a successful book these days.

You can co*mmit to the tracking approach.* Do a set amount; even if it's only 30 minutes to an hour each day builds a cumulative effect. You could write 1 chapter per week and have a short book in 7-12 weeks.

16. **Write overcoming writers block.**

    Writers block can be a serious hindrance, especially when you only have a small window to work on your book. Here are a couple of tips to get rid of writers block anytime you face it. *Know you don't have to write chapters in order.* You can jump around and fill in the blanks to gain momentum. *Maintain your momentum.* Don't give in to writers block. Move on to work on the chapter you feel passion bubbling for at that moment.

17. **Write a short book.**

    Because your book is shorter and easier to write fast, you can expect to go to market sooner. To accommodate your weekend writing, write your book in chunks, chapters, sections and parts.

    Writing this way will allow you to easily refine, repeat and repackage your information. You'll be able to synch your book with a website and pull out a stream of articles, reports, follow-up products and even services to build your book, your brand and your business.

18. **Write using the q/a format.**

    Make a list of 7-10 burning questions or problems that you have collected from your clients. Write an introductory or overview chapter. Then take each question and answer it in an individual chapter. Pad your chapters with a case study, a real story or an illustration to explain the answer. Write a closing chapter, review everything and congratulate your reader for finishing your book.

19. **Write with a chapter template.**

    You need a shell to just slip your book content into. Using a chapter template as a shell is similar to building your best crispy taco. You bake (form) the shell and start putting your meat in; then add lettuce, tomatoes, cheese, sour cream, etc. until you have built your best taco.

After creating a book chapter template, you can easily see where your introduction, 7 supporting points, stories and summaries fit into each chapter.

20. **Get a professional editor and/or a book coach.**

    Yes, its o.k. and you should get feedback from family, friends, local writing group, etc. But you need to get a professional viewpoint of your work to weed out the passive voice, bad grammar and all the things that slow your readers down to a standstill. Copy that appeals to the emotions of your reader sell your books. Your future customers want word pictures that they can respond to with their emotions.

21. **Brand yourself, your business and your book.**

    Think about the greatest benefit that you offer through your book or service. Consider your book and chapter titles. Now think about your keywords and headings on your website. Do you see a repeating word that stands out?

    For example, the book "Win With the Writer Inside You" the author threads some form of "win" throughout her materials. Ever heard of the Chicken Soup for the Soul series? The title changes in its audience but the Chicken Soup brand stays the same. For example, there's a Chicken Soup for Teen-agers, Chicken Soup for Mothers, and so on.

If you don't use the principles above to write your book in the small blocks of time available to you, you may never finish this year. I'm casting my vote in your favor as a fellow weekend writer. I believe you can do it!

You don't have to say I can't because I don't have time anymore. You have the knowledge; you can now say I CAN. Go make us all proud; write your book in the midst of your busy life with the time YOU have, even if it's just on the weekends. See you at the finish line. Finish fast; finish strong and sell sooner.

THIS WEEK'S ASSIGNMENT

1) What 3 speed tips can you implement now to speed up writing your book?

___

___

___

2) If any, what myths did you recognize as 'your wrong thinking' about getting your book written this year. What steps will you take to change your thinking and take action?

___

___

___

P.S. Don't forget the personalized coaching positions that are available at http://www.bookwritingcourse.com/roundtable.htm (If nothing else, you may want to invest in the first month if you need help in getting your book off to a great start.)

WORDS WORTH REMEMBERING:

Success is the sum of small efforts repeated day in and day out.
—Robert Collier

Coming Up Next ...

Chapter 11: *How to Write Compelling C.H.A.P.T.E.R.S.*
In the next chapter, I'll show you how to write compelling chapters fast and an invitation to access the 1 page book proposal report shortly follows. Yes, prospective self publishers you still have to write a 1 page book proposal in this course. Trust me; it will do much more for you than you think but at the least it will help you crystallize your message.

CHAPTER 11

How To Write Compelling C.H.A.P.T.E.R.S.

If I speak in the tongues of men and of angels, but have not love, I am only a resounding gong or a clanging cymbal.

—1 Corinthians 13:1

Well done! You are almost to the finish line. I hope this course has set you on an undeniable path to the completion of YOUR book. I invite you to offer feedback about the course. A few days after the final lesson, if you signed in online I will send you a survey and a free gift if you complete it for me.

Also, based on previous student feedback I am continuing to revise this course to make it better and better. Anytime, I complete a revision I will notify my student list and let you know about it.

But before all that, don't tune out before receiving the final lesson and bonus report. In lesson 12, I'll cover some subsidiary products you can develop from your book. And in the companion bonus report I offer instructions and tips on how to create one of the most requested products in my business (hint: it was created from my book) along with sizeable discounts on related products.

I did my best to fill this lesson chock full of good information to help you write compelling chapters; so let's get started...

HOW TO WRITE COMPELLING C.H.A.P.T.E.R.S.

Is your book organized? The best non-fiction books are organized like a paved road guiding readers through their chapters. That paved road of organization includes mile markers, exit signs and other road markers for each chapter. Think about it; we easily get lost unless the path is clear. It's stressful to take a journey without a clear road to travel.

Most people enjoy a journey (even a book journey) on a paved clearly marked road. Instead of leaving your readers to follow a mucky path of disorganization through your book, use the formula below to create a can't-miss-it road like the yellow brick one in the 'Wizard of Oz' movie (1939).

I use the acronym "C.H.A.P.T.E.R.S." to describe each of the necessary steps for writing a chapter(s) in your book:

C – CHOOSE your chapter topic.

H – HAVE a purpose for each chapter.

A – ARTICULATE your main message/thesis.

P – PRESENT the supporting points.

T – TELL the relevant details to entertain and educate.

E – ENGAGE your audience to make them participants.

R - REACH a formatting decision to organize your book.

S – SUM up your chapter and polish like a professional.

Let's take a quick look at each of the EIGHT steps...

1) CHOOSE your chapter topic.

Every lesson begins with determining what you're going to write about for that specific chapter. As a general rule, there should be ONE primary focus in terms of your chapter topic. What will you write about?

I'm sure you have many ideas by now; but I want to give you four more quick ways to find ideas (and/or research for filler material) to write about that you can use for any of your chapters...

.. *Competitor's book TOC.* That is, you find an existing book that is related to yours and you look at their table of contents. Usually this will inspire many ideas to use as topics for your own chapters.

.. *Magazine cover stories*. Another method is to look at the covers of magazines or feature articles related to the topic of your book. You can cover the same topic with your twist or insight on the subject. This will also yield ideas to write about ... and fresh ones come with every new issue! (Note: You can also check your library for past issues or hunt for them online)

.. *Bookstore lists.* Drop by your favorite bookstore (or browse online for even greater convenience at Amazon.com or BarnesAndNoble.com) and search for more books within your category/topic and look for (1) The subjects of the books themselves and, (2) additional ideas in the table of contents or on the back covers.

.. *Ezine article subjects.* You can also visit your favorite online ezine article directory (EzineArticles.com, GoArticles.com, etc.) and look within categories related to your topic for existing ezine articles. Many of these will serve as suitable ideas to build chapters on.

Even after encouraging you to use this method, I must remind you to do this to find IDEAS. Certainly, you don't want to copy their material or even use a similar format or structure in organizing your chapters. Just use these methods to brainstorm ideas to write about.

2) HAVE a purpose for each chapter.

Decide what you want your reader to do after reading each

chapter. Are you explaining a step in a process? Or are you telling a story? To keep your book's main topic and the content of each chapter focused, make each chapter one complete thought or idea. It should be able to stand alone.

People have different ways that they read and digest information. One reader may be attracted to read chapter one first and the next reader may start with another. Therefore, you want to capture their attention no matter where they start. You stand a better chance of getting your reader's attention when you write well purposed chapters or compelling copy.

3) ARTICULATE your main message.

To best communicate your main message, write your chapter in sections from the template in the previous chapter. Start with *an Introduction:* Begin each chapter with 6-8 paragraphs of introduction. The introduction may include a short story presenting the chapter's main principle or underlying thesis. For short books 3 to 4 paragraphs work best. You don't want your introduction to over power your chapter.

Then Create an opening statement: For example, you could open each chapter with a thought provoking question or a startling statistic that show where your audience is now (before reading your book.) Many authors begin with a short analogy or story. Whatever you decide to open with, create an attention getter to hook your reader.

Prepare a thesis statement: After your short introduction including your hook (opening statement), write your thesis. Keep it simple; let your readers know what benefits await them if they keep reading. For example, one author friend used sizzling bullet points to entice the reader into the chapter. You may place them right below quote or directly below introduction.

4) PRESENT your supporting points.

To present your supporting points, create the appropriate list, steps, ways or questions and answers that you'll use as the foundation for your chapter.

• If you are going to use a "list" in your chapter, then share as many as you can possibly think of—even up to ten or twenty. Also, if you are sharing "ways" or "tips" or "ideas", the more you can share the better. Why? You'll soon discover not all of the ideas will be relevant or interesting to the individual reader. But, if you include several ways to do xyz, it's likely one or more will hit the target and keep your readers happy.

• If you choose "steps", then I recommend single digits. The more steps there are to complete, the less likely your reader will actually do them. Aren't we all like that. In this case, less is more. Keep it to 9 steps or less, preferably 3-7 steps.

• If you are going to use "questions", then I recommend that you keep it to 10 questions or less. For the same reason, less is more when it comes to making it easy for your reader. It's important that you organize your questions in the simplest way so they are chunked together by topic.

I encourage you to share at least 2-3 tips or examples for each of your major points. My readers send me love for this one. Most people appreciate as many different perspectives on information as possible. (Try it; you'll get love from your readers too!)

Even with this lesson, take a look back at the first three steps that we've covered so far ... most of them have additional "sub-points" that further clarify or illustrate the major points.

After you have presented your supporting points, it's time to...

5) TELL the relevant details.

TELL the details of your chapter. Use case studies, stories and illustrations. Remember to use the points and sub-points that you've mentioned in your outline or table of contents. If, you write 1-3 paragraphs for each of your points/sub-points, you should end up with a basic but meaty chapter.

But wait don't stop there! Don't you want to write compelling chapters that practically force your readers to keep reading to the end of the book? Don't you want to set your chapters apart from your less informed competitors? Here's what I have discovered, most people read books for two basic reasons. When you intertwine the 2 elements I'm about to tell you about into your books, you will begin to reel your readers in like fish on a hook.

One of the basic reasons people read a book is they want to be entertained. Most of us, if not all of us, enjoy a good story. It's like in the movie 'Out of Africa' starring Meryl Streep and Robert Redford. In the movie, Ms.Streep's character captivated her friends with her stories. Jane Austin's books made into movies continue to be remade & reborn because of her story telling abilities. Even, the National Enquirer and other tabloids get a lion's share of readers with stories like the 6 armed alien that captured Madonna one night.

Secondly, readers want to be educated. Especially, non-fiction and self help books attract readers that want to learn something. Not only that, but they want to learn it in the easiest fashion with the least amount of steps as possible. For instance, a new mother wants to learn what to expect when her baby becomes one, two or five. Or a small business owner wants easy steps to set up a money making website. Whatever your readers want to learn and you are ready to teach, remember people read to be educated.

So how can you make your chapters entertaining but educate your readers at the same time? I'm so glad you asked. There are some specific techniques that you can use to accomplish both of those goals at the same time.

Let's start with entertainment. I've listed 5 methods you can captivate your reader's attention through entertainment:

• *Use analogies.* An analogy is when you compare one thing with another. Earlier, I could have said you can intertwine 2 basic elements to make your book more interesting. Instead, I said, "When you intertwine the 2 elements I'm about to tell you about into your books, you will begin to reel your readers in like fish on a hook." Or if the writer said, "How would you like to write an ebook that many people can't wait to buy?" instead of "Want to write an ebook that your readers stampede like a herd of cattle to read?" Which of these sounds more entertaining to you?

• *Develop Acronyms.* This is one of my favorite ways to entertain. Why? Not sure why, it just feels like successfully filling in a crossword puzzle. And all the cross word puzzle lovers say, "Yes!" I knew you would understand. (smile)

Anyway, using an acronym, you organize your content by the first letter of a word. Did you notice? I used one in this lesson. C.H.A.P.T.E.R.S. In my lesson, I used the words Choose, Have, Articulate, Present, Tell, Engage, Reach and Sum to explain the parts of this lesson. The acronym entertains; but it also makes your material easy to remember.

• *Tell a story.* In my marketing material, I often use a story about how I started writing books. I am transparent with folks about some of my struggles. Some of my most popular articles and reports have been how I made a mistake or struggled and eventually found a solution I wanted to share.

I practice 2 Rs in telling my stories. Be relevant and be real. Make your story relevant to your chapter material. And be real in your expression. In other words, you don't have to make up stuff or pretend like you're someone you're not. Use your real life examples and stories; you'll connect much easier with your audience.

• *Be humorous.* Humor goes the extra mile to entertain. If

you want to lighten the mood of your reader, don't be afraid to insert some humor. No, I'm not saying you should try to be a comedian throughout your book. I'm just saying it will give your material the feel that a real person wrote it and you're talking to a real person. Well placed humor will help you to entertain and connect with your reader in a compelling way.

• *Hint at revelations.* An easy way to draw your reader in deeper is to hint there's more to share or more coming in later chapters. Give a little preview; then say you'll explain later. Our news media and show producers use this technique all the time.

Remember all the shows that you've heard, "Don't go away; we'll be right back with that interesting story, Up next we'll show you how to..." Building anticipation grows excitement. Create excitement with anticipation; then make sure you don't forget to make good on that promise later in your chapter.

Next we'll cover 3 major ways to build education into your chapters. Your readers will love you for it.

• *Deliver action steps.* Newbie authors miss the mark with this one. They offer their reader the steps but in no particular order. Your readers get frustrated if you don't give them the proper steps to follow in the right order.

Most of us want a detailed, chronological list of what to do and when to do it to accomplish a task. Make it simple; make it easy for your readers and they will come back for more and send their friends to get your book.

• *Give application.* How do I apply that to my life, to my work is one of the most asked questions. Therefore, give your readers examples, instances, ideas, samples and case studies to help them apply the principles of your book. Your audience loves to see the results. Results move people to action. It touches the place in us that says I want to do that too! It worked for them; maybe it'll work for me.

• *Offer Tips.* Put in as many tips as you can muster up. In fact, all your left over nuggets and miscellaneous material (related to your book) compile into tips and put in the back of your book. Or consider giving away a free booklet or ebook of tips to promote the full length book. You can develop tips with a list of keys, tactics, techniques, ways, methods, options and much more.

I hope you got some good ideas on entertaining and educating your readers; because now you're ready to set your chapter up for action.

6) ENGAGE your reader audience.

Use engagement tools to pull your reader in and compel them to act. Create active participants of your book readers using engagement tools like worksheets and note sheets. Make lists, questions to ponder or boxed tips to actively engage your readers instead of allowing them to be observers. *Add self-evaluation tools like* brief questions that permit your readers to measure their progress with each of the principles described inside the chapters.

There are so many different "angles" to engage your reader. (q-tips or the fastest way to do something, ways to improve, logs, journal space, note space, shortcuts, schedules, questions, exercises, mini-lessons, side bars, pull quotes, etc.) that you could mix-n-match and never stop coming up with ideas to write into your next chapter. After deciding what engagement tools you want to use, get ready to organize your chapter.

7) REACH a formatting decision.

Next, you'll want to decide how you'll organize the content of your chapter. While there are many different methods of doing this, I personally recommend one of the "big three" when it comes to sharing information in a book…

.. List. A list is simply that: a set of ways, tips, keys, suggestions, ideas, methods, techniques, hints, etc. (I.E. 21 Book Title Templates. Remember that?)

.. Tutorial. A tutorial is a set of chronological steps to complete a process. If the topic of your chapter can be described in "how to" format, then it is a tutorial and should be organized in sequential steps. (Most of the lessons in this course are arranged in this format.)

.. Q&A. A "questions and answers" format is used when you identify a series of key questions related to your topic and then provide answers to them. (You can solicit questions from your audience; answer them and insert in your chapter.)

After you have decided which of these three formats works best for the chapter you're about to write, then get ready to finalize your chapter…

8) SUM up your chapter then put finishing touches on it.

Summarize your chapter. Each chapter may end with four to eight paragraphs that summarize the central idea and supporting points. Or you can use 1-3 if your book is short. Don't forget to hold the carrot out at the end: Build anticipation by inserting 1-2 sentences at the end of your summary to entice your readers with benefits waiting in the next chapter.

After you've written the content for your chapter, you'll want to fine-tune it. Generally speaking, there are three things that I recommend you do in putting the finishing touches on your chapter...

.. PAD. Fill in; look for areas of the chapter that need further explanation. Are there any areas that are not clearly explained? Are there areas that are noticeably weaker than others? Make sure your points are understandable. Try to add in as many examples or stories as possible to better illustrate the points. Put in a few more tips here and there where needed.

For example, in an earlier lesson I started out with 10 book title templates. But I kept looking and found other title tips that I had written and could add until I had 21. You can insert interview transcripts, quotes, research and other bits of information to get the points across better and add a bit more meat to the chapter. Now is not the time to skimp. Do your best to over-deliver in your book.

.. POLISH. Use different fonts to distinguish areas of your chapter content. Change colors. Use alternative styles such as bold face, italics and underline. Indent text where appropriate. Use bullet points; especially use on lists. Insert headers, footers, clipart and graphics (just don't overdo it!)

.. PROOFREAD. The final professional touch you want to make certain you do is to proofread your entire document for typographic and grammatical errors. Better still; allow someone else who is qualified to do it for you. While this isn't a deal breaker by any means (quality of content is MUCH more important than quality of grammar in information based chapters) Even so, it's a good idea to make your manuscript as professional as you can.

NOW ABOUT YOUR FIRST C.H.A.P.T.E.R.

The formula for writing a chapter is perfect for ALL of your chapters, but I want to give you a quick tip about the content of your FIRST chapter. Without question, most people in general want quick results. They don't want to wait a year, six months or even one month. They want results quickly.

So, it's important that your very first chapter be a "quick start" chapter that gives your readers something that they can immediately do in order to see some kind of results. Unless your book is specifically for newbies, give your advanced audience and beginners both something to be excited about.

I recommend the following schedule for most non-fiction books...

.. *Chapter #1* is an "overview" chapter which explains the overall process that your book is devoted to.

.. *Chapters #2-5* are "explanatory" chapters which explain the basic steps of completing the basics of the overall process.

.. *Chapters #6+* are "refining" chapters which explain various details on enhancing and expanding the overall process.

Step out of your comfort zone and create a yellow brick road for each chapter. Use the simple formula C.H.A.P.T.E.R.S. above and before you know it you'll have written a compelling book that your customers are flocking like birds to read. Enjoy the journey. Life is made easier.

THIS WEEK'S ASSIGNMENT

1) Write 1-3 sample C.H.A.P.T.E.R.S. using formula above.

____

____

____

2) Write a query letter and 1 page book proposal for your book. Don't forget you can use some of the passion point results from earlier lessons and exercises.

____

____

____

3) Decide whether you will self publish or pursue traditional publishing. If you are pursuing traditional publishing, purchase a *Writers Market Guide* of your choice and look up a publisher in your market and send a query letter. If you are self publishing, read the *5 Point Self Publishing Checklist* as a first step.

P.S. Don't forget the personalized coaching positions that are available at http://www.bookwritingcourse.com/roundtable.htm (If nothing else, you may want to invest in the first month if you need help in getting your book off to a great start.)

WORDS WORTH REMEMBERING:

Your decision to be, have and do something out of ordinary entails facing difficulties that are out of the ordinary as well. Sometimes your greatest asset is simply your ability to stay with it longer than anyone else. —Brian Tracy

Coming Up Next ...

Bonus Report: *How to Build Multiple Streams of Income*
In the final lesson, I'm most excited about teaching you to make money from your book before it's published but especially after it's published. Just these principles alone in the bonus reports are worth the cost of the whole course...

CHAPTER 12

How To Build Multiple Income Streams From Your Book

In the morning sow your seed, and in the evening do not withhold your hand; for you do not know which will prosper, either this or that, or whether both alike will be good.
—Ecclesiastes 11:6

Thanks for reaching this lesson! I am so proud of you. I'm happy you are 12 lessons plus closer to achieving your goal of writing a saleable book. I suspect it wasn't one of the easiest things you've ever done. At any rate, I offer you the chance to let me know how you progressed or not through a short survey in a few days. I'm grateful for the opportunity you gave me to pour what I know out to you.

One of the final steps in the book writing program includes refining, repeating and repackaging. It involves developing and continuing with a website, a stream of articles, reports and follow-up products and even services to build your brand further. Once you capture your reader's email addresses and permission to keep in touch with them, you'll want to develop an ongoing stream of articles and even new information products to sell them.

Also, in an ongoing basis you want to review your modules of information and nuggets of information and chunk it into shorter articles and columns which you will promote with everywhere you can online and in print. Your main goal in submitting articles and columns is not to gain income but opportunities to expose your book website URL and sales letter to potential visitors.

Use informational articles and reports. People are online majority of the time looking for free information. Your article can be comprised of a single idea, or a brief overview of the contents you cover in a chapter. Columns interpret more than educate. They permit you to give your opinion on current trends, events or outside influences affecting your readers.

The more exposure you and your website receive the more your credibility builds to support you as an expert and author in your field. Producing your articles for promotion will become easier and easier as you invest time in chunking your knowledge and information.

Email newsletters offer you another opportunity to keep in touch with your readers. Your newsletters can be either informational or opinionated. Either way, they give you an opportunity to remain visible and build even more credibility.

Be sure to include your case studies and testimonials to further promote your competent service or product.

Technology has advanced making it easier and easier to electronically publish your own e-books. The profits from each sale on a per-unit basis can be 10X the royalties earned by your original book. The growing possibilities of future income and promotional opportunities are articles, columns, white papers and special reports, journals, workbooks, newsletters print & online, coaching and consulting.

Though your goal may not be to be a publishing-machine putting out best selling books to formula but it is important to consider ways to partner with your readers through your website. You can continue to produce articles, books and updates that help you profit from your passion. Each new related material further reinforces your credibility as an expert.

HOW TO BUILD MULTIPLE INCOME STREAMS FROM YOUR BOOK

Would you like to create life long passive income? Income streams that produce like the Energizer™ bunny, going and going and going. You can do it; just use the principles in this program, to write, complete, publish and create multiple income streams for you and your family.

Even after you finish your book manuscript new ideas will probably continue to surface. Ideas that you wish you had thought to include in your book. Instead of going back to re-work your manuscript consider using them in your promotional or marketing material. Become a trusted resource and supplier of fresh information in your field.

Continue to develop your topic by creating articles, speeches, workshops, courses, or invite readers to submit questions and suggestions to your website. Develop your topic and title into a brand that produces increasing amounts of income through your personal services and/or information products.

To create your own brand with multiple income streams start with these ten tips:

1. **Promote passionately while you write.**

Many authors and especially small business owners/authors dread book promotion like a plague. With all that I already do, I jumped the hurdle of writing and completing my book, now I have to promote it as well –arggh.

Yet, book promotion is not an activity most publishers are accomplished at either. You, as the author - the one who believes - the most in your message, have to take responsibility for promoting your book. Publishers are like factories producing printed books or distributors delivering boxes of books to bookstores. So don't believe the myth that a publisher is going to promote your book.

Unless your name already has tons of acclaim, most publishers will do little or no advertising of your book. They may send out a limited number of press releases and review copies but often depend on the catalogs they send out twice a year to bookstore buyers.

In an interview when asked about the success of his last books, Spencer Johnson whose book "Who Moved My Cheese" stayed on the best seller list five years after its release with more than 14 million copies sold and counting said, "The economies of book publishing allow a book publisher to actively market a book for 30 to 90 days, then it depends on word of mouth.

It's not just the agent or the advertising, though those things help. In the end, the book has to resonate with people's hearts and heads." With all that in mind, it's no surprise why your publisher is more than likely not going to be able to do your book justice and the real promoting will fall to you. You have more to gain than the publisher in the success of your book.

During the planning stage of your book don't forget to include the passion points designed to sell your book. One of those passion points is to identify and contact the influencers in your field. As early as possible, send them your book's table of contents and two sample chapters.

The two sample chapters and table of contents help prove your commitment and intention to complete your book project. Make it one of your top goals to have a "name" or trusted authority in your field endorse your book by either providing a brief quote or testimonial for the front or back cover.

One good way of approaching an established authority is to interview them. This establishes at least a dialog with them. In the process of interviewing, at the opportune moment you can ask for a quote or even an overview/introduction for your book project.

Some might ask for a symbolic honorarium but most will be pleased to write a brief overview or testimonial for your book project because it further promotes them in their endeavors. Beyond quotes, your book marketing plan should include a list of review copies of your book for possible mention, review in their publication or website.

2. **Synch your passion filled book and website.**

In your pre-planning your website should be built into your book as frequently as possible. If not already, begin to view your website as an equal partner with your book and not just another way to promote or sell your book. As early as developing your title don't forget to consider how well your title converts to a website URL. Create a separate website address for each book(s).

One of the best ways you can synch your website and book into partnership is to offer one, or more, free sample chapters. Develop an ongoing partnership between your website and the contents of your book.

For example, if you are including worksheets and/or note sheets as a reader involvement tool you can mention that readers can download an electronic version of the worksheet from the website. Building your website into your book from the beginning makes it easier to develop secondary income streams later.

Be open to learn from your reader's comments and questions. Invite feedback, whether positive or negative, look for the lesson it contains to improve your relationship with your readers.

3. **Contribute Articles**

One of the best vehicles of promotion is writing articles. Take your original book content and create an article. According to the size of your book, you may be able to slice several articles out of its content. Following this program, you can easily excerpt nuggets or chunks of information for your article.

The best place to start with submitting your article is your own website. You do have one, right. There's no better place to launch your multiple streams of income than from your website.

A client of mine wrote a book about how to create an e-book called "6 Ways to Multiply Book Sales with an E-Book." His articles might include: 20 Ways to Increase Sales with an E-Book, 8 Ways to Write a Winner e-Book Fast, and 18 Reasons to Write an E-Book and Give it Away Free.

Each article was easy for him to create for he simply excerpted a block or chunk of information from his original book. Without re-writing, he simply cut & pasted the information and repackaged it into an article.

Similarly, if one of his book's chapters was on web promotion, he could easily excerpt his original ideas and develop the topic further in a series of articles presented by his original chapter: Five Good Reasons to Publish an E-Book, How to Sizzle Your E-Book's title to Sell More, Why Use an Ezine to Promote Your E-Book.

4. **Become a Frequent Speaker**

As a published author, you can develop a profitable speaking career. If you enjoy travel this is one stream of income well worth developing. Published authors can command a fee for their time and input.

Whereas, unpublished writers are limited to speaking for free or a limited fee based on their expertise in their field. Speaking as much as you can will help you achieve several goals as author:

- Confidence. When you first start out, speaking may not be one of your strengths. You'll find just like anything else the more you do it the more confident you will become.

  It gets easier and you will communicate more effectively. Before long you will be excited about your speaking trips instead of viewing it as a dreaded book promotion duty.

- Promotion. Each speaking engagement will promote your book. Each speech will build your portfolio for future projects with your publisher.

Additionally, every engagement will build your credibility a little bit more in your reader's eyes. Be sure to post your engagements to your website.

- Website Content. If you create a PowerPoint visual, a transcript, tapes, or video of your presentation, be sure to post it on your website. It continually builds you and your book website as a resource.

It will build additional credibility by offering your visitors and clients a sample of your speaking and information.

5. **Publish Your Own E-book.**

You will receive your advance and royalties from your original book. But everyone that knows anything about traditional publishing knows you will receive only a few cents on the dollar.

With e-books, you can create and sell directly from your website at full selling price. So as you excerpt portions and repackage your book, always look for ways to develop topics you can sell yourself.

For example, an author has written 7 Steps to Operating a Successful Home Business. There are several e-book topic directions the author could follow:

- Market Segments. The author could direct e-books to specific markets, i.e. stay-at-home moms who own a home business, Successful Home Business Solutions for *Stay-At-Home Moms* or *For Dummies*. Another target market could be Successful Home Business Solutions for Medical Professionals.

- Economic Trends. The author could consider creating an annual update based on economic conditions, i.e. Home Business Solutions During a Recession, Home Business Solutions When Times are Tight.
- Problem Solvers. An e-book topic could be based on symptoms, i.e. Home Business Solutions for the Budgeter, Home Business Solutions on a Shoestring, Home Business Solutions & Time Management.
- Techniques. E-book topics could be developed from a technique for a targeted market: i.e. Taking Your Home Business Online, Home Business Solutions Using Your Computer.

Another category of e-books could develop with downloadable checklist, worksheets, templates, and case studies: i.e. 15 Push Button Easy Home Business Plan Templates.

6. **Become a Resource to Your Readership**

I remember an associate of mine that I and many, many others turned to whenever we needed to know something. To us, she seemed to know everything.

When one of us asked what to do with our children during the summer, she delivered a list of top things kids can do while their parents are at work. When someone wanted to attend a church closer to their home, she supplied a list of churches in their area. She was a resource to all those around her.

As you continue to develop and grow your topic information, new ideas will continue to emerge. The same resources you used to support your topic while writing your book can be repackaged into a valuable product. Not valuable because its new information but the fact that it's all in one place ready to be used for a specific purpose makes it valuable.

For example, one of my colleagues published a list of 40 or 50 paying writing markets in his e-mail newsletter. His list developed into targeted markets for Christians, travel, women, men, etc.

He sells his carefully researched 50 Paying Market list for 5.99 each. He already created the list in his research for one of his books. He now just has to check links and revise annually.

7. **Subscription newsletter or website**

After you have begun to establish yourself as an expert by writing and publishing your book, have built an email-list full of people that are interested in your topic and want to hear from you, you could consider developing your information into a subscription medium.

The more specific, targeted and sought after your information the greater your success will be a paid subscription newsletter or website. As with the e-books, you don't have to be concerned about creating print copies. Your only job is to provide fresh content about your topic on a regular basis, usually weekly or monthly.

8. **Expand Your Services**

After 9-11 events, travel has become less attractive to some. As an alternative, many are turning to tele-coaching and consulting. Tele-coaching includes creating one-on-one relationship with readers to help them achieve their goals.

Tele-coaching allows you as a published author to mentor another individual without traveling or office-visits. In a weekly, usually one-hour telephone calls to consult with your reader helping them achieve their goal.

Offer Tele or E-Courses. While developing your book, you might consider building in ways to convert it into a course. A telecourse or e-course is another couple of ways you can excerpt and repackage your knowledge over and over again. The required reading for your telecourse includes your book plus a series of PDF files which you send out at weekly times.

Telecourses usually consist of weekly one-hour telephone calls and last from 4-12 weeks. Course participants call a central, typically rented, telephone number called a bridge. Each participant can hear the course leader plus every other participant.

Members can send e-mail to all the other participants by sending a single e-mail to a list serve, which is often available for free from websites like http://www.yahoo.com. Each week's phone call is based on discussion of new course material and written assignments.

The number of class participants usually range from 5-40. After the class protocol has been set, everyone gets a chance to speak. Tuition can range from $49.00 to $1000 or more according to who the author is.

E-courses or e-Mail Workshops are similar without the aspect of the phone. You would still take your excerpted knowledge from your original book and develop lessons that are sent via email.

The numbers of lessons usually range from 5 to 12. You could develop a short lesson to include in your email or provide a link in your email directing the student to a PDF version of the lesson or a html page.

E-courses or tele-courses allow authors to leverage their knowledge and yield yet another profitable income stream from a world-wide market. A typical tele or e-course may attract participants from Europe, the Middle East and Asia as well as your local town or region.

9. Offer your book for pre-ordering

If you are self-publishing, you can offer a pre-release version as an ebook for sale. Or you could set a date for publishing and pre-sell copies then mail them to customers as soon as you receive your first shipment. You might be surprised at how customers will pre-order your book and wait patiently to receive it.

Writing your book can be a rewarding and profitable journey. Use the *Write Your Best Book Now* book writing program and course to excavate and organize your ideas, identify your passions, and write a successful book faster than ever. Then use the book in your program to explore and leverage more profit streams than you ever imagined.

THIS WEEK'S ASSIGNMENT

1) **Choose 3 subsidiary products** you will develop from your book?

____

____

____

2) **Outline your plans** to develop at least 1 of the above products?

____

____

____

P.S. Don't forget the personalized coaching positions that are available at http://www.bookwritingcourse.com/roundtable.htm

WORDS WORTH REMEMBERING:

If one advances confidently in the direction of his dreams, and endeavors to live the life which he has imagined, he will meet with a success unexpected in common hours.

—Henry David Thoreau

Coming Up Next ...

Bonus Report: *How to Turn Your Book Into An Ebook*
In the following report, we'll discuss how to develop one subsidiary product (ebook) from your book.

BONUS REPORT 1

How To Turn Your Book Into An Ebook

A man can receive nothing-except as it has been granted to him from heaven. (a man must be content to receive the gift which is given him from heaven; there is no other source)
—John 3:27

Congratulations on officially completing the Book Writing Course! You can consider this lesson and the next your graduation gift.

No, there really are no more assignments. The ball is in your court now. I encourage you to keep going with your writing whether you successfully met the goal of writing a book in 100 days or not. As a Christian there are always higher heights and deeper depths.If you completed your book and the course was a help to you, write me and let me know. If you haven't finished quite yet, don't lose heart. Take the course over again or just keep going; you'll get there.

I want to finish with some valuable information that helped me decide and take action after finishing my manuscript. Don't forget to drop me a line or two to let me know how it went in the course. Or simply fill out the survey you'll receive in a few days. Thank you, again. And best wishes for your success as an author!

HOW TO TURN YOUR BOOK INTO AN EBOOK

You have a wealth of information about your field. You have already written a quality book for your audience. Here's another way to make your book go the extra mile for you. You can develop your book excerpts into short ebooks or simply use your full manuscript and offer an electronic version.

If you need additional help developing the electronic version of your print book, you may visit http://www.ebookitsuccess.com for the *eBook It* epackage designed to walk you through each step to launch your ebook online.

Using free ebooks as a method of promotion is reaching peak popularity. If you thought book signings, flyers, paid ads and brochures were the only way to prime the pump for book sales, think again. You can take sections of your book and convert them into short ebooks or easily convert your book manuscript into an electronic version book (eBook.) Here are some tips to get you started:

1. **Should I offer free ebooks?**

You may initially have concerns about giving your ebook out free. Here's the key principle. Unless you are already a well-recognized name in your field, your free ebook is worth much more to you in free publicity. If you do decide to offer portions of your book as a free ebook, another thing to note, is to not make it an encyclopedia. Save some for when your audience actually buys your book.

In other words make it useful but incomplete. I made that mistake with my first ever ebook. It was an inspirational title in a tiny niche market. I compiled a free ebook from book excerpts to promote the print book. It pushed my subscriber rate way up but hardly anyone was buying. It jumped from 2 or 3 to 10-15 to now about 50 or more sign-up per week. Anyway, as soon as I figured out I was giving away too much and withdrew some information, my subscribers started buying.

If it's for paid publishing this rule does not apply. Don't hold back. But if it's for free publishing, offer enough to entice your audience to want to know more. Offer your ebook as an overview of what your audience would learn about in its fullness in your book or paid information product. As a way of developing my books, I usually create a chapter that gives a complete overview of what's in the book. This includes a paragraph or two explaining each chapter. I target this chapter as my gift – my free sample chapters, report, free ebook or even my free mini-course.

If I am using a free report, my audience will be directed to go to my website where my book is being sold to get the full treatment of my topic. Or they will have to sign-up for my free ezine to get the full story (again where they are exposed to my book ad.) So don't be hesitant, give first and you shall receive (book sales.)

2. **Review your book chapters.**

Look for a topic that you can pull out and entice your audience with. Then add an introduction and ending to compile your short ebook of about 5 to 30 pages.

For example, in my first print book I mentioned earlier I went chapter by chapter and pulled out my favorite sections. (The favorite sections of my book just happened to be some of my most well written and passionate writing.) I added a short introduction, ending and voila some of my most popular ebooks were born. You can do the same for your book.

Later go back through and look for underdeveloped topics. A point you briefly covered in your book but you could easily write more to develop a short ebook to promote your book. Perhaps, you already have some excess material from your existing body of knowledge or research that didn't fit into your print book. You could easily compile this information into an ebook.

3. **Sizzle your title.**

Create sizzling titles designed to hook your potential readers. One of the most important skills to develop as a marketer of your book is the skill of creating attention-grabbing titles. When you master this skill you may use it in every aspect of your writing to attract more readers, more sales, and increase your profits.

You needed title writing skill for your book titles, chapter titles, sub-heading and now article titles. Even bullet points will have pulling power if they are developed correctly. Your website will need passionate headings to capture the attention of your web visitors. Title well and sell well.

4. **Design your ebook for quick reading.**

Your audience is hungry for information. But they want it in the right format. The format must be easy to read, easy to digest and easy to apply. Quick tips, question/answer, how-tos, and problem/solution are good styles to start with.

Your audience will love your easy to read information. They will reward you by reading every thing you publish. They will even visit your website, sign-up for your ezine, free ebook and eventually buy your print book just to get more of your helpful information.

5. **Proofread and edit your ebook.**

I assume you have already edited or had the information edited for your print book. But it's a good idea to edit it once again after revisions for your ebook. You don't want to risk detracting from your credibility by promoting with an ebook full of errors.

Don't forget to use your skills at your highest level and outsource the rest. If you are not that skilled with editing, don't hesitate to pass your manuscript on to a professional editor.

6. **Include a signature box.**

Develop your signature box into a compelling ad for free information that will lead to wherever your book is sold. Allow your prospect to find out more about you through your short ebook. After reading your helpful ebook they will be more open-minded about buying your book.

7. **Convert your MS Word doc file into a PDF.**

You can create your ebook by converting it into the popular PDF file. The PDF (Portable Document Format) was created by Adobe®. It has become a universal format that preserves all of your original formatting. Not only does it maintain your specified layout, but it also preserves your fonts, images and links -- regardless of what application you use to create it. This enables your ebook to look exactly as you formatted it to look.

Additionally, PDF files are compact in size and are smaller than their original source files. They are easily published and distributed in a numerous ways: Print, Email attachments, Download (online), Web sites and CD-ROM.

Now, if you want to simply create a paid version ebook out of your full manuscript you would go on to:

7. **Setup your direct response website or webpages**

There are several different models of websites that you can setup for your book and e-book. All the experts agree the best model to use is the direct response website. The direct response website is what some have termed as a *mini-site* that's setup simply with limited options.

On this mini-site, you don't want any distractions. You only want your website visitors to focus on your book offer. Normally, the DR min-site has its own domain name, a one page sales letter on the home page, order page, an affiliate page (optional) and an email capture form.

8. **Create a way for your readers to purchase your book online.**

Setting up your payment system is a necessary function of selling your ebook (information product) online. But it doesn't have to be as hard as it may sound. In fact, it can be as easy as a one time setup with very little ongoing maintenance.

Free enterprise has advanced. It used to be very expensive to get a merchant account. There are now many professional companies on the Internet which are ready to help you get setup.

If you are not ready for a merchant account there are also numerous 3rd party companies that will process your orders for you. All you need do is link your web site to their secure servers. Payment processors like iBill, PayPal, ClickBank, Revecom, 2Checkout.com are ready to serve you.

In order to profitably sell your ebooks or other information products on the Internet, you must accept credit cards. Additionally, to sell effectively, you must make the ordering process as simple as possible for your customers. With the advance of technology and free commerce, even the smallest home business or author can now accept credit cards almost instantly.

9. **Generate targeted traffic**

Here's where some people get stumped. They jump the hurdle of writing a saleable book then getting their direct response website setup but they are clueless as to how to advertise their site. For you see, it doesn't matter how wonderful your book or mini-site is if no one knows they exist

It's important that you focus on quality advertising and book marketing methods. The methods must be one that connects with people that are interested in the book you're offering.

The biggest mistake unseasoned book sellers make is wasting

time and money on unworthy advertising methods. Most FFA (free for all) link site, traffic exchanges, safelists, ad blasters are not worthy of your time.

If you invest in time waster advertising, you'll only get burned out after getting very little in return. Instead, choose the proven ways to get targeted online traffic – both no cost and low cost.

There are lots of books and information products written on this subject. But one of the most effective ways of letting people know about my books has been Article Marketing. For me, using Article Marketing has turned a drip flow of book sales into a steady stream. If you want to know more about using article marketing to promote your book, visit http://www.articlespeedway.net for details.

Now that your ebooks are ready free or paid, begin to promote them everywhere you think your targeted market searches for information on the Internet. Your short free ebook filled with insightful information and your signature file becomes the ad for your book.

Along with all the other places you submit your ebook, setup a page on your website. The more information you circulate, the more your exposure increases along with your book sales. May your book journey become even more successful with an ebook.

WORDS WORTH REMEMBERING:

Don't wait for your ship to come in and feel angry and cheated when it doesn't. Get going with something small.

—Irene Kassoria

Coming Up Next ...

Bonus Report: Self Publishing 101

The next week's bonus report is designed to offer you tips to make a knowledgeable decision about self-publishing.

BONUS REPORT 2

Self Publishing 101

Now go, write it before them on a tablet, and inscribe it in a book, that it may be for the time to come forever and ever.
—Isaiah 30:8

Have you joined the halls of self starters finishing your book with speed and accuracy? If so, congratulations! Now is the time to prepare your book for successful self publishing. The preparation step of the self-publishing process includes everything you need to do to your book manuscript before you deliver it to the book printer. This includes deciding your publishing goals.

For example, is your book a personal family history book that you plan to sell to a few friends and family? Or do you plan to mass market your book to the world?

STEP ONE

SELF-PUBLISHING EDUCATION

As with any business venture you must educate yourself to have the best possible chance of success. There are lots of misinformation and misunderstandings of self-publishing in general. Education is a powerful piece of the 'Success Pie.' You wouldn't dream of becoming a book writer without first learning about book writing.

The aspect of Book Publishing is no different. This book

about Self Publishing is one of the best starting places for your publishing education currently being offered to the self publisher. Remember, Knowledge is Power. If you are reading this ebooklet, your self publishing education can start here.

Know your options. Discover the difference between vanity publishers, subsidy publishers, book packagers, pod publishers and self-publishing.

The term *vanity publisher* in general, refers to the publisher (sometimes called a book producer) who prints and binds a book in medium to large quantities at the author's sole expense.

On the other hand, a *subsidy publisher* considered (a joint venture publisher, a co-op publisher, or a partner publisher) also takes payment from the author to print and bind a book. Unlike the vanity publisher, they may contribute a portion of the cost, as well as adjunct services such as editing, distribution, warehousing, and some degree of marketing.

Book packaging is different than subsidy or vanity publishing. Some companies as their business specialize in it. A book packager serves as an independent contractor to produce a predetermined number of your books. All the books belong to you. Book packagers work for a pre-set fee, and all the profits are yours.

POD publishing is exactly what it says: Publish on Demand. This means that books are printed when someone orders them, and they aren't printed unless someone orders them. After the books are printed and sold usually quarterly the POD publisher pays the author royalties from their book sales. They aren't stocked (except in minute quantities) in distributor warehouses. Which is for the most part a good thing except when bookstores look them up on their databases they often find that they have to be "backordered?"

The term *Self Publishing* is most commonly used to discuss publishing that is handled completely by the author. Self-publishing requires the author to undertake the entire cost of publication him/herself. The writer would handle all marketing, distribution, storage, etc.

It must be made clear; self publishing implies that "you" are the "publisher". In fact, ownership of the ISBN determines who the publisher is. If you didn't buy your ISBN's directly from RR Bowker, you don't own them. If you do not own the ISBN, you are NOT considered a self publisher in the publishing world.

STEP TWO
SELF-PUBLISHING PREPARATION

The preparation stage of the self-publishing process includes everything you need to do to your book manuscript before taking it to the book printer. This includes determining your publishing goals. Like do you plan to sell your personal family history book to a few friends and family or do you plan to mass market your book to the world. After deciding your market then you prepare your book using the important steps below:

1. Write a business plan

This is where book publishing journey begins. Remember, you don't have to start with a 30 page document. But do draft an outline of all the costs that you will have in the self publishing process.

Include costs before publication, after publication and everything from start up costs to the shipping price of mailing a book. This is the point you decide whether you should purchase a single ISBN; print a small quantity of books for friends and family or establish a small publishing company by purchasing a block of ISBNs.

2. Get ISBN numbers.

Remember this is what identifies you as a book publisher. It is the only way you can be considered a self-publisher in the publishing industry. At the time of this writing, no one can give, assign or sell you ISBNs except RR Bowker, the U.S. ISBN agency or their approved representative.

3. Invest in book editing.

Invest in your book; get it professionally edited. Copy or line editing will bring your manuscript up to professional standards. Don't settle for having your family member take a look at your manuscript.

4. Hire a book designer for book layout.

The book layout is what structures the content of your book and makes it look like a book. Again invest in your book project, this is not the time to settle for any thing less than a professional look. If your book looks sloppy, it will limit its success in the market.

5. Consider do-it-yourself layout options.

If your budget is a shoestring or you are a die hard do-it-yourselfer, you might consider purchasing a book template software like Book Design Wizard (see the Resource Rolodex at the end of this book.) You simply input your text, images, book specs and the software will generate a professional layout for submission to your printer.

6. Thinking of other do it yourself layout options

If budget is not a major concern, then you may consider investing in Pagemaker or InDesign software for your book layout projects. The price is a little steep at $400 to $699 at Adobe's website. Also, you may encounter a learning curve but there are good templates that will shorten it for you. Either way you decide, make your book the best it can be. Your readers will love you for it and proudly refer your book to all their friends.

7. Create bound galleys for reviews.

Bound Galleys are limited run book proofs, often unedited, generally used to get book reviews before the publication date of your book. Additionally, bound galleys do not have a laminated full color cover.

8. Get your book proofread.

Some are tempted to skip this step in preparing their book for publication. My advice is don't skip this step. A book full of errors can cost you in sales later on--including loss of respect for your work.

Proofreading is not the same as editing; it is done after the book designer formats or lays out your book into pages. The proofreader looks particularly at word breaks and sentence layout. Some minor corrections missed in the first line edit may also be made.

9. Invest in cover design.

Seventy-five percent of 300 booksellers surveyed (half from independent bookstores and half from chains) identified the look and design of the book cover as the most important component.

They agreed that the jacket is prime real estate for promoting a book. On that note, your book cover design can make or brake your book marketing campaign. So, I encourage you to get your book cover professionally designed.

10. Considering do it yourself book cover options.

We know not to judge a book by its cover. Yet, we all do it. So realistically, a book is judged by its cover in the publishing world. If you want your book to have the best chance of success in a professional market, don't drop the ball here. Another option for the do-it-yourselfer to get a professional look is the *Book Cover Pro* software (see the Resource Rolodex at the end of this book.)

STEP THREE

SELF-PUBLISHING BOOK PRINTING

According to how far along you are in your self-publishing process, you may know this already. Most printers can print books although most printers are not book printers. With that said, the question becomes can they print your book in a way that's cost effective for you.

Additionally, don't forget to consider the option of direct pod publishing with Lighting Source, a subsidiary of Ingram. You essentially submit your fully prepared book to them for printing and some distribution. See Chapter 7 page 48 for the details. I've listed below some options for your book's trim size.

SINGLE COLOR TRADE PAPERBACK AND HARDCOVER -
Standard Book Sizes

Mass Market Paperback – 4¼ X 7"

This trim size used to be called dime novels. Because the large publishing houses print this size in tens of thousands it's tough to compete in small quantities. Also, the perceived value of this size is lower than the other book sizes. Choose this size cafefully.

Trade Paperback and Hardcover – 5½ X 8½"

Its the most popular trim size for fiction and non-fiction books. If you are planning for a quanity above 500 copies it doesn't make any difference whether you use this size or the trade paperback alternate size of 6 x 9. If you plan to print quantities under 500 copies, choose this trim (actually 5¼ X 8¼"). It is significantly less expensive than the 6X9 alternate with no lower perceived value.

Trade Paperback and Hardcover alternate – 6 X 9”

This was considered the standard trade paperback size for years before the Internet printing press. This size fits perfectly on a 25 X 38 standard size sheet of paper. This is now the standard Internet printing press book trim size. If you are printing quantities above 500 copies, this is the recommended trim size.

Textbook Paperback and Hardcover – 7 X 10”

This is considered standard size for text books and other “how-to” books. It is best in quantities above 500 copies because it fits the Internet printing press perfectly. Under 500 copies yields the same pricing as 8½ X 11” only you trim off the excess paper.

Workbook – 8½ X 11”

It is considered a standard workbook trim size. Printing under 500 copies you’re dealing with a slightly smaller trim size (8¼ X 10¾) because of the digital equipment standards. Over 500 copies fits traditional Internet printing press. Its hard to compete with large publishers in this size for the same reason as the Mass Market size.

Color Illustrated Paperback and Hardcover
Illustrated Children’s Books, Art Books, Travel and How-to Books

Hardcover and Paperback 8 X 8”

Standard children’s book size. Not recommended for paperback children’s books in low quantities. The competition is too tough from traditional children’s book publishers. OK size as hardcover children’s book or as paperback for non-illustrated children’s books. Pricing is available with or without book jacket.

Hardcover & Paperback 8 X 10"

Very standard children's book size. Like the 8 X 8, not recommended in paperback for children's illustrated books. Pricing is available with or without book jacket.

Hardcover & Paperback – Oblong 10 X 8"

Standard children's book size. Not recommended in paperback for children's books but great as hardcover. Common paperback size for non-children's picture books. Pricing is available with or without book jacket.

STEP FOUR

SELF-PUBLISHING DISTRIBUTION

At the time of this writing there are no perfect distribution channels for the self-published book. Looking for the perfect book distribution channel is like searching for the pot of gold at the end of the rainbow.

Unless you have a detailed marketing plan and a good amount of money working for you, and in many cases, access to media and traditional bookstore distribution, you may be headed for disappointing sales. Don't get me wrong; I'm not predicting you won't be successful. But I am saying it will most likely be like swimming against the tide trying to distribute and market books in a traditional manner.

Here's another good reason to consider POD publishing or printing your book through the Lighting Source company. Your pod published book will be included in the Ingram database as a POD title. This one program will make your book available to a network of 20,000 retail stores including Amazon.com and BN.com. This inexpensive distribution is a good starting place for getting your books in the bookstores.

STEP FIVE

SELF-PUBLISHING MARKETING

Push Button Easy Book Marketing

Ready to get those books stacked in your garage into the hands of even MORE readers? Earma has harnessed the power of internet promotion into one place to set your book ablaze with new sales. Get the ebook Push Button Easy Book Marketing Strategies with software bonuses that help you promote your book to a new market - the WORLD. www.bookmarketinghelp.com

1001 Ways to Market Your Book

If you haven't done so already you need to buy a copy of this book. Some of the information is a little dated but for under $30 it is a great place to start. www.amazon.com

Book Author Website Design

This is a must if you have any hope of being successful selling your self published book. It's your way of telling the "world" about your book. These days, after the initial setup you can get author web sites for as little as 9.95 per month. www.scriberecreative.com

Online Bookstore

The perfect "first step" for selling your book on the Internet. List your book in available online book stores.

Social Media and Blog Tour Campaigns

Including Internet marketing is a must in the technology age, we live in. At time of this writing, you should start with the main top four social media Twitter, Facebook, Youtube and LinkedIn. Research the top blogs in your field of ministry area and contact them to consider guest appearances or articles about your book's topic. And don't forget the hundreds of Internet radio shows and websites that you can promote your book. Each have its own share of subscribers and visitors.

Press Release Service

Promote Your Business with Professional and Affordable PR Services including placement on News. Google, Yahoo!, Reuters, and thousands more, starting at only $69! Visit Send2Press.com for details.

RR Bowker/Book Marketing Works

Direct Sales to the non-bookstore market. They generate the leads and you make the sales calls or they generate the leads and they make the sales calls. Visit http://www.bookmarketingworks.com/ for details.

Are you ready to successfully publish your book? Did you consider all your options including a business plan and book cover design? Great! Now that you know how to prepare your book for full speed ahead self publishing, go ahead take the plunge. Don't hesitate any longer. Start today. Your audience is waiting for YOUR unique message and viewpoint. Make it different. Make it count. Make it yours.

WORDS WORTH REMEMBERING:

Be daring, be different, be impractical, be anything that will assert integrity of purpose and imaginative vision against the play-it-safers, the creatures of the commonplace, the slaves of the ordinary.

—Sir Cecil Beaton

WABGW Book Writing Commitment

I [ ] prayerfully dedicate the next 100 days of my life to writing a book manuscript while using the resources I have to use (right now).

Print Name

Sign Name Date

Begin to act boldly. The moment one definitely commits oneself, heaven moves in his behalf. –Gerald R. Ford

25 Strategies to Writing Your Book to Success

Jumpstart Checklist:

Based on the "Lessons" allotted for each of the earlier exercises, it will take you approximately 6 weeks total time. But if you are writing your book part-time, weekends or along with a full time job like I had to do with my first book and several subsequent books, it may stretch out over the quarter or approximately 100 days.

<u>Date</u> <u>Goal</u>

1. _____ Make a commitment. (Ch. 1)
2. _____ Develop writing schedule. (Ch. 1)
3. _____ Select a saleable book topic. (Ch. 2)
4. _____ Target your book reader. (Ch. 2)
5. _____ Write a plan. (Ch. 3)
6. _____ Write 1-2 sentence book thesis. (Ch. 3)
7. _____ Write book introduction (bonus lesson)
8. _____ Compose back cover sales message. (Ch. 4)
9. _____ Design 60 second billboard. (Ch. 4)
10. _____ Develop book's selling (passion) points. (Ch. 4)
11. _____ Develop promotion plan (Ch. 5)
12. _____ Test your book's significance. (Ch. 6)
13. _____ Create a sizzling title. (Ch. 7)

14. _____ Research and/or compile info. from files. (Ch. 8)

15. _____ Organize your book ideas. (Ch. 8)

16. _____ Develop the book's table of contents. (Ch. 9)

17. _____ Create a chapter template. (Ch. 9)

18. _____ Discover how to write your book fast. (Ch. 10)

19. _____ Write a sample chapter. (Ch. 11)

20. _____ Write rough draft. (Ch. 11)

21. _____ Edit using the Quick Self-Editing guide. (Bonus)

22. _____ Re-write, fill in holes and polish final draft.

23. _____ Write 1 page book proposal. (Bonus)

24. _____ Checklist for self-publishing. (Bonus)

25. _____ How to build multiple products. (Ch.12)

100 Day Fast Track Module

Week 1: Use quick start techniques early; choose tracking method.

Week 2: Get to know your potential reader; write chapter 1.

Week 3: Write plan for your book; write chapter 2.

Week 4: Write your selling points; write chapter 3.

Week 5: Plan book promotion; write chapter 4.

Week 6: Test your book's significance; write chapter 5.

Week 7: Develop title writing skills: write chapter 6.

Week 8: Organize info from your knowledge, research; write chapter 7.

Week 9: Create a toc & chapter template; write chapter 8.

Week 10: Use techniques to finish faster & write chapter 9.

Week 11: Write sample C.H.A.P.T.E.R.S. /rough draft; write chapter 10.

Week 12: Plan multiple streams of book income and write chapter 11.

Week 13: Create 1 info product from your book; write chapter 12.

Week 14: Self-edit and polish manuscript; consider publishing options.

Sign up for the *BookWritingCourse.com* membership site and receive important reports *The Magic of the 100 Day Timeline* and the *Book Title Tutorial and Templates.*

About Author

ɞ

Earma Brown lives in Northern Texas with husband Varn. She is a 15-year author, book writing coach, and web developer who helps Christian service business owners, writers and infopreneurs write, publish and market effectively their books. She has a Bachelor of Science degree in Business Administration and has completed graduate work in Communication.

CONTACT INFORMATION:
Earma Brown
P.O. Box 180141
Dallas, TX 75218
http://www.earmabrown.com
http://www.writingabookgodsway.com

Other Books & Resources by Earma Brown

Book Writing Course - 12 week course (online)

Get started today with 12 week course (3 months) & receive FREE Paperback. (limited time offer) Additionally, during the course you will receive extra bonus reports (at least 1 each month) including *100 Day Timeline*, *How to Write a Query & 1 Page Book Proposal* reports for further instruction to get your book done with speed and excellence. Visit http://www.bookwritingcourse.com

Self-Publishing Power Box

Tired of waiting to get published? Why not take destiny in your own hands. Get the book *Self-Publish Now* & discover how to self-publish, POD publish & market your book with less time, less effort & less money. Stop waiting to get noticed by the 'Big Guys.' Join the ranks of other successful self-starter publishers. http://www.selfpublishyourbooknow.com

How to Write a Winning Book Proposal

Would you like to GET PAID to write a book? If you're thinking this is plain fantasy, think again. All professional writers get paid to write their books. How? They sell their books via proposals before they write the books. *How to Write a Winning Book Proposal: Get Paid to Write a Book* gives you a complete method. The e-book shows you EXACTLY HOW to write and SELL. Write to Win Shop http://www.writetowin.net

Article Marketing Speedway

Discover how to get more FREE traffic the easy way. The *"Article Marketing Speedway: Putting Your Articles in the Fast Lane to Sales"* will show you step by step how to write short articles that sizzle and have everyone publishing them faster than cars racing in the Indy 500! http://www.articlespeedway.net

Ebook It! How to Profit From Your Passion Using Your Information

Are you looking for a way to turn your knowledge into a profit center? The experts finally agreed on something. Creating an e-book using your information is the fastest and most profitable way to make money online. Earma Brown's *eBook It!* system and bonuses will increase your brand awareness, help you become an expert in your field, and earn money while you sleep. http://www.ebookitsuccess.com

40+ Article Writing Templates

Download the mega pack of *40+ Article Writing Templates* & 21 article samples from author Earma Brown! The templates offer you a jumpstart on writing short easy articles fast. Also, these are the same templates Earma uses to promote her products and services to profit every week. These article templates include title suggestions and a step by step guide you can use every time you write or only when you need a jumpstart to fast article writing. (40+ article writing templates, article submission software, 80+ article title & content prompters and 21 sample articles.)

http://www.40articlewritingtemplates.com

READY FOR TEAM TRAINING?

The Armorbearer Training Series bundle of books gives you the insight and tools needed to develop a strong chain of support in your local church team. Together leaders and supporters may bring in a more fruitful harvest. Buy one for every leader and/or supporter in your church! Visit http://www.theshieldshop.com for bulk discounts:

ISBN: 978-0-9797701-3-5

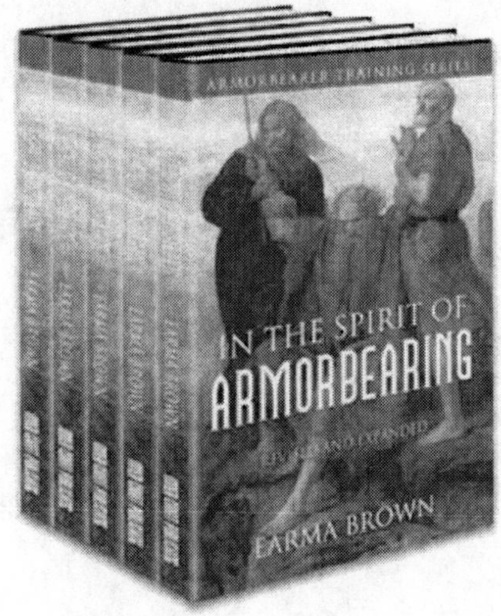

In the Spirit of Armorbearing (original paperback)

Wondering where to start your study? The *In the Spirit of Armorbearing* book (paperback) was designed just for you. Get your copy today and get started! (revised and expanded too) **$12.99**

In the Spirit of Armorbearing Study Edition (paperback)

The *In the Spirit of Armorbearing Study Guide* (paperback) has been written to help you fulfill your call to effectively help God' leaders as servants of Christ. Earma presents and challenges you to apply biblical armorbearing and ministry of helps to your life of service. She utilizes a simple 5 step process to guide your personal study or your small group study. **$14.99**

RESOURCE WEBSITES:

Book Writing Coach Services
http://www.writetowin.org
http://www.100DaysToABook.com
http://www.bookwritingcourse.com/roundtable.com

Author Services
Book Cover Design, Book Editing, Websites
http://www.scriberecreative.com

Book Publishing
http://www.butterflypress.net
http://www.selfpublishinghouse.net

Notes

Notes

Notes

CPSIA information can be obtained at www.ICGtesting.com
Printed in the USA
LVOW06s1013230114

370651LV00002B/657/P

9 780979 770173